INTRODUCTION

The reason I have decided to write this book is because I had a great response from people who read my first book, Growing up in Northfield, which was about myself, my friends, and the things we got up to.

"Back in the days" if you needed to sort out a grievance you would name a time and a place. Most of the time you would turn up with your friends and the other person would turn up with their friends (just for moral support). It was always one on one, no weapons just head, fists, and feet. After the fight was over there was sometimes a handshake, win or lose.

If you had a dispute inside a pub or club you would normally just go around the back of the pub and sort it out! most of the time after the fight was over, you would go back into the pub and have a drink together, over and done with! Nowadays most of your fighting and bullying is done behind a screen (keyboard warriors) and can go on for days, weeks and even months.

Over the years I have had the privilege to know some of "Aberdeen's hardest men and women". After some research, it has given me the opportunity to speak to some of them that I had never met or spoken with before, and to find out their background and history.

My own experience growing up from an early age and into my late thirties, I earned myself a reputation for being a bit of a scrapper in my area and in my local, The Lord Byron. The reason for this was, I was bullied for years as a kid, mainly because of my size (overweight short arse!) until one day, I had enough. I just snapped and started to fight back until I earned some respect and was never bullied again.

Looking back my Father and Grandfather were never fighters so that was my theory out of the window, because I always thought that with hard-nuts it was a genetic thing.

After conversations with some of the people mentioned in the book, most of their stories were familiar with my own. They were bullied from a young age, some of them started out as boxers, or their parents and grandparents were well known hard-nuts.

Some of the stories that have been written are either my own or other sources opinions. Probably everyone will have their own opinion as to who was "Aberdeen's hardest".

After reading this book some people might be asking themselves oh, "why wasn't he or she not in the book?" but after a year's research, I have approached many people to find out their stories and background. A few of them were very reluctant to have their stories in the book which I understand and completely respect their wishes.

Some of the names in the book only agreed to it because I have known them personally for many years. In my opinion and probably most people reading this book will agree, that at one stage in their lives they were "Aberdeens hardest", but the book is about who was the hard-nuts in their area of Aberdeen. This is an argument that could never be resolved as you will always have the up and coming next generation after your crown to make a name for themselves.

I have always said that it doesn't matter how hard you are, there is always someone out there harder than you. I never forget the old saying *"always look out for the quiet ones"*.

CHAPTER

1

Names of men that are featured in the book and known as some of 'Aberdeen's Hardest' over the last fifty years.

A.Lawson

J.Moir

Brown Brothers

B.Sutherland

J.Gill

D.Gribble

S.Moore

Turners

A.Gibson

N.M^{c}lennan

G.Moore

J.Robertson

B.Laing

L.Hutcheon

B.Macrae

ANDY LAWSON
(R.I.P)

A boy who knew Andy Lawson told me a cracking story. His words were, "Andy Lawson was the hardest man to walk the streets of Aberdeen."

A big-name Glasgow Gangster by the name of "Gypsy", John Winning, who was transferred to Craiginches from another prison. He had quite a reputation and all the other Glaswegians were very wary of him. As soon as he arrived, he made it clear that he was going to run the show and nobody else should even think about doing so, "especially that Bam Lawson." A big comment to make and one not ignored by the local guys in at the time.

A few months later, Andy Lawson got nicked for non-payment of fines and was jailed. When he arrived at Craiginches prison, the local guys weren't slow to tell him what Winning had said about running the jail and how he was expected to tow the line!

Andy turned the TV over and Gypsy shouted from the top landing, "Hoy you, turn that back!"

Andy shouted up, "Shut the fuck up or I will come up there and batter you!"

Gypsy said, "Up you come".

The guys watched on as Winning made his way back to his cell. Within minutes, Lawson headed for Winnings cell, he wasn't in there more than fifteen seconds when he strolled back out and went to his own cell. No sight or sound of Winning, so somebody went up and looked in... Next thing, the medical staff were heading up to Winnings cell with the screws. About twenty minutes later Winning appeared at the door supported by two screws, with his eyes both split and his head about twice the size it should be, both eyes were completely shut and the size of "Co-op baps". Gypsy ended up in the hospital wing for a week.

That was the end of John Winning running Craigie.

This guy who wished to remain anonymous didn't kick about with Lawson, but knew him from the Looking Glass Pub and said he was a solid guy.

Andy was in jail on three occasions with Glasgow's Jimmy Boyle and never a crossed word between them. An old acquaintance of his from Woodside, who had been in jail with him, told me, he was most certainly a "One-Off". He knew Lawson well from drinking in the Millers Bar in Woodside and from prison. According to him, Andy didn't really have any visible knuckles, it was just one long, thick solid ridge of bone and like a sledgehammer hitting you.

Lawson got a mention in the book about Johnny Ramensky, the safe-cracker and prison escapee. The top guys, including Lawson, were all sitting at a table in Barlinnie with all the big Glasgow Gangsters including Tank McGuiness. McGuiness was last seen outside Parkhead one night with John Winning before he was found murdered. Obviously Winning was the prime suspect but they couldn't prove it was him.

Lawson was getting money monthly from Bobby Morrison, the

bookie. Protection money if you like, and it seemed Morrison was getting fed up handing over the money to Lawson, so one day he decided that he wasn't going to pay him any longer. He used to hand over the money in the Silver Slipper pub on Rosemount. On the payment day, Lawson arrived at the pub and Morrison was standing there with this "man mountain" of a guy, Crombie overcoat, leather gloves, the full ticket! Lawson walked over and said, "Have you got my money, Bobby?"

Morrison replied, "That's all stopping as from now Andy, I can't afford to keep doing this"

Lawson said to him, "Bobby, give me the money and don't be daft!" suddenly, the "man mountain" pushed Morrison aside and said to Lawson in a cockney accent, "Did you not hear the man? he says........" That was as much as he got out of his mouth, as Lawson goes, CRASH! CRASH! and hit him with two unbelievable punches. The first one knocked him out and the second was just for good luck, but he was sparked before he hit the floor. Morrison looked down at his minder, lying unconscious on the floor and knew his plan was fucked!!

Lawson said to him, "Bobby, have you got my money?" Morrison reached into the inside pocket of his jacket and handed him a brown envelope and said, "Here you go Andy, I thought that might happen".

JOHN MOIR

I never ever got in to any bother at school but was always fighting with folk from other areas when I was out of school.

Later, in life I started to get a bit of a reputation and that's when it all started, as it seemed like someone always wanted to have a go at me.

I was always loyal to my mates and when someone started with any of them I would always get involved and sort things out for them, but that's what friends are for.

After a while, I started to think "fuck this" I was always getting into trouble with the police. I had just started a family and couldn't be arsed with that kind of life, fighting, and getting into trouble.

We drank down at Woodside, we were made welcome there because my dad was very well known down that area, he was also the Doorman in the Tanfield for a while.

I was in Jumping Jacks night club when this guy bottled my mate thinking he was on his own. He thought he was it, because he was with a few of his mates, but he didn't realise I was with the guy he hit with the bottle. As the guy walked past us I said, "fuck you!" hit him with a left and knocked the fucker out! This other guy came over and crashed me, next thing, the bouncers were in the middle of us and the both of us got thrown out the back door.

As soon as we got outside I was on top of this guy giving him shit, and this guy started biting my arms and legs, I thought *Fuck You!* I can do the same, so I took a bite out of his head and ended up with a mouthful of his hair. Next thing his brother came out screaming that he was going to stab me. This passer bye said, "the cops are on their way you better get off of him," there was blood pissing all over the guy. I helped him up and said, "fuck we better get out of here!" we were walking down John Street to the Ambassador club to clean ourselves up a bit in the toilets. The guy went to phone his mother to come and get him. His mother turned up and he said to her "give my pal a lift home as well," driving along and his mother was giving him shit "who the fuck have you been fighting with?"

The guy said, "that fucker in the back seat, but just take him anywhere he wants to go."

One time when I was just a youngster walking up Union Street, some older guy put the head on me and then ran away, I chased after him, but soon lost sight of him. This other guy came up and started laughing at me because there was blood all over my face. I said, "Is that fucking right now?" so I put the head on him, then his mates came running over. I smacked the first one and while he was falling to the deck, I went to smack him again. Well, I missed and fell right on my face, another one of his mates came running over and put the boot into me, but I managed to get up and went crazy, so they also took to their heels.

One of the stories a few years back that I just about got jailed for, was when me and my mate were doing a pub crawl along the harbour. We walked into the Crown and Anchor Bar and as soon as we walked in this "huge, massive" guy grabbed my mate from behind, put the head on him and burst his head wide open. After he did that he looked over to me, blew me a kiss and then started screaming at me, "C'mon then Big Boy!" So out came Val, the barmaid and said "come on you lot calm down and please no fighting in my bar" she then took me around the back of the bar, she sat me down until I was a bit calmer. After about ten minutes I was wondering where my mate was, I ran outside and noticed the blood pissing down from his face. I looked up the road and saw the guy with another two guys and their wives at the bottom of the Shiprow. They looked down at me and started shouting, "C'mon! Big Boy! do you want the same?" I ran up towards them and the only thing that separated us was a fence in the middle of the road, I hit the cunt and he just hit the ground like a ton of bricks. I then jumped over the fence and the guy that stuck the head on my mate threw a punch at me, I ducked, and he missed me, so I smacked him and as he started to fall back he twisted his legs and his head crashed off the ground, and that was him out cold.

The third guy grabbed me and said, "calm down," so I gave him an uppercut and he was also out cold. I looked down and these three guys were lying out cold all over the road. Two of them looked in a very bad way. We got out of town as quick as we could as the police were out looking for us.

Next day, I got rid of all my clothes and shoes as they were covered in blood. Cops came up and lifted me, I ended up in court the next day. I got three hundred hours community work which took fifteen months to complete.

We were in the Byron one day, we were just young and this guy I knew from school came over and said, "Moir my mates in a bit of trouble outside"

I went outside to see what was going on, next thing this little cunt took a swipe at me, so I decked him. Then this other guy came running down, who was very well known for being a "hard-nut", by this time, the wee cunt got up off the deck, they grabbed my phone and jacket and took off. I ran after them and challenged them both, but they ran off. When I stopped and turned back they would stop and challenge me, but same again I turned around and they ran off again. I was thinking '*how I was going to catch them'* so I hid behind a door and as they passed me I jumped out and ended up knocking this hard-nuts teeth out.

A few weeks later I was sitting in the Fountain Bar waiting for my mate Dotty. He walked in and said, "there's a few folk outside wanting a word with you," I was wondering who the fuck it was, so I went outside and standing there was the guy whose teeth I knocked out with two of his mates. He said to me "are you John Moir?"
I said "yeah, why?"
He said, "you're the guy that did this to me," before he said another word I said "why? do you want some fucking more like?"
He said, "No! No!" then shook my hand and left.

I mind when I was fifteen years old and drinking in the Metro, these two girls I knew were arguing with some guys. I was sticking up for them and this well-known hard-nut from Torry came over and headbutted me, so I knocked him over and, on his way down I volleyed him in the mouth. The bouncers came over and the guy told them I glassed him, so I got thrown out. Waiting outside for me were a group of Torry boys, well, "In for a penny, In for a pound"...... I got torn into the lot of them.

A mate of mine got a right doing over in this pub from two grown-up men, well that was me getting stuck in again. I ended up fighting with them both. I even ended up with their footprints in my back. Just young and naïve, I picked up a glass ashtray and belted them with it. When I got home and told my dad what I did, he battered me for using an ashtray.

I was in the Broadsword bar one night and was as "pissed as a fart". When we left to walk home we started walking up Mugger's Bridge. Suddenly, this guy came walking past us, at that point I was walking behind my crowd and the guy started shouting at me, he then pulled a knife out, so I grabbed him and started smacking him off a lamp-post. The guy started groaning, (I probably went a bit overboard with him because of the knife,) next thing, Coppers arrived and started to chase me. I was running down the bottom of Poundstrechers' car park, when I got to the end, I couldn't go in any further because there was a wall. I was thinking, *what the fuck am I going to do,* as the Cops were closing in on me. Not having much time left I jumped clean over the wall and fuck me there was about seventeen feet drop at the other side. I knocked myself out for a moment, I then looked up and all I could see were the Coppers looking down at me lying on the ground. They shouted down, "fuck you! we're not climbing down there to get you!" and they just left me there. "Another lucky escape for me".

One thing that used to get me going were the bouncers in town, One night I was outside standing in this queue to get in and it was pissing down of rain, when we finally got to the door the bouncer said I wasn't getting in, I argued with him "why the fuck couldn't you have said that hours ago when you saw me standing in that queue?" I ended up fighting with him, I picked up a beer keg and bounced it off his head.

At a bar in town, my mate came over to tell me that these two guys approached him and said, "wait till you get outside, you've had it!" at that time, I had to watch what I was doing so, I said to him, "Ok! come outside with me when I leave and see if they do anything." We got outside and started walking down Union Street, we looked around and the two guys were following us, Like I said, I couldn't get into trouble because of my ongoing court case. I said to my mate, "get into this bus stop and see what they do," in they came and started with us, so knocked the first one out, started to walk away and at that point, I was out in the open, the other guy jumped on me and started swinging round my neck like a monkey. He kept hitting me, I was saying to him "I canna hit you back as there's CCTV, but get you, and your mate down this lane and I will fight you both!"

By that time the rest of my mates came out the bar, the two boys ran across the road, as some of their mates had appeared, so me, "like a bam" ran across the road to get to them. I ended up getting torn into them and once again they ended up running away.

John and his father
Graham

I have known John since he was a kid, he used to help me deliver milk at weekends with his pal Dotty. People tell me now that he has grown up, he has followed in his father's footsteps as he was one of Aberdeen's hardest back in the days.

THE BROWN BROTHERS

The "Battling Brown Brothers" which were very well known, "back in the days", you had Alex, Brian, Thomas, and James.

Alex was the oldest out of the four brothers, they were very well known around the boxing scene. One of their greatest achievements was that the four brothers held six North-East and Midlands titles between them at the same time.

Alex was the last one to start boxing as he was away doing his National Service. Brian was the first to start boxing at the age of eleven, Brian joined the army in 1954 and won all his Scottish Command Championships.

Brian also fought Aberdeen's Legendary Johnny Kid. They were called the 'Mighty Titans' on the billboards. Brian was the quiet one out of the four brothers, his elder brother Alex always said that Brian was the best boxer out of the brothers.

When Brian came home on leave from the army he found out his mother had no money to feed the family (it was hard times back in the days). Brian decided to go down to the boxing booth at the fair, to win some money for his mother. Unfortunately, someone reported him and that was his career as a boxer finished.

"I knew Alex and Jim from my days in the Millers bar and had many a laugh with them. I would say they were Aberdeen's hardest but also gentleman."
-Lynette Allan

"Great fighters, I saw them on many occasions, they used to box down at the Aikie fair. These were fixed fights and boxed for money, which was the reality in them days. People were poor in them days and boxing was a way for them to make a few pounds, nothing glamorous about it but happy days"
-Douglas Brown

in Pleasure Park

On WEDNESDAY, 14th JUNE, 1961.

Commencing 8 p.m.

10 EXCITING CONTESTS!

D. McTAGGART, Dundee
Olympic Gold & Bronze Medalist

G. Ross, Inverurie A.B.C.
Fly Weight

J. BROWN, Aberdeen
Light Weight
North Eastern District Champion

The family lived at the Castle Hill Barracks before moving down to Woodside. Jim was the manager of the Tanfield bar in the seventies which saw some of Aberdeen's hardest walk through their door. You got the odd one or two who came in looking for trouble.

Just up the road from there was Miller's bar, Alex was the bouncer at that time. One day these three well-known men went walking in looking for trouble again, just as they did on previous occasions. Alex had enough and sorted the three of them out BANG! BANG! BANG!

The Brown Brothers never looked for trouble, only if it came their way. At that time, they were great boxers and never exploited it. Alex always said he wasn't a bouncer, he was just a barman that assisted in throwing people out.

"Tommy taught me to box, and every other Saturday round the back of our tenements we would have boxing matches. The winner got all the empty bottles the neighbours had collected. Good times and a really nice family, even now I always talk about Tommy."- **Tom Donegan**

I knew the Brown Brothers well. Back in the 80's when me and my hubby Nipper Brown ran the Summerhill Lodge, Alex Brown was a regular at the bar.

One-night Nipper and I got a night off, so we went over to the Cocket Hat for a drink with another two members of staff. The four of us were enjoying a quiet drink when this guy came over and smacked Nipper on the side of his head, the reason being, Nipper gave me a kiss on the cheek and this guy said, "we are not having this in here," well, Nipper not one to let things go, went up and grabbed the guy by his tie and smacked his head over the bar. Well, all hell broke loose and this guy

15

and his mates jumped on Nipper. I ended up with a broken nose and Nipper had a few cuts and bruises.

When Alex heard about it, he and his brother Jim went out to find them. When they did, they did some damage to him and told the guy to move out of Aberdeen pronto and never come back, he left right away and has never been seen in Aberdeen again.

"was out with my dog one day in Hazelhead Park, when my dog decided to jump a barb wire fence and caught its bollocks on the wire. My first thought was to run across to the swimming baths to see my uncle Tommy, out he came with this bottle of Dettol and cleaned the blood off my dogs' bollocks. Wish I had a camera then LOL."
- **Roy Brown**

Brian had a friend called Harrigan. One day they were driving out in the country in Harrigans' van. When suddenly Brian told him to stop! He then jumped out of the van and started running across some fields, he later came back with this Piglet. Harrigan said, "you're not fucking coming in my van we that thing!" and locked Brian out of the van. Eventually he let Brian in the van but without the piglet. All the way home, all Brian could think of was this little piglet on a tray with an apple in its mouth.

Brian was driving down Clifton Road just behind the Northern Hotel with his wife Liz and their kids in the back. Brian noticed this guy outside the hotel looking at them, he said "this cunt is up to something". As he approached the guy he stepped in front of the car causing Brian to slam on his breaks. Brian got out of the car to

confront him and the guy started giving it all mouth, so Brian, pinned him to the bonnet and punched ten bells out of him and threw him back on the kerb.

Brian is typical of all real Hard-men, a big gentle giant until you upset him.

"when we got called up into the forces I went to the Army and Tommy went into the Air force. One night on leave me and Tommy went out and decided to change uniforms for a laugh, not one of our better ideas, as we were stopped by the military police and ended up in trouble again. Tam went on to work at Hazelhead swimming pool in later years."
- George Wood

Jim ended up getting six months in jail for acquiring some leather jackets. At that time in the seventies there was this guy on TV who had the same jacket and he was a bit of a "jack the lad" Jim was selling them by the dozen.

Jim was also the bouncer at the Cheval Casino along with another hard-nut Dick McGregor.

"I remember my mother telling me a story about my uncle Robert Ogg and the Browns. It wasn't long after the war and they stayed above 'Woollies' in George Street. One night she was lying in her bed when she started seeing boxes of sweets and chocolates going up past her window LOL."
- James Walker

BRIAN SUTHERLAND

Brian was brought up in Manor Avenue. As a kid he had a rough upbringing but wasn't a fighter, he was the complete opposite.

One day at Hilton school these two boys beat him up and he didn't even raise a finger to protect himself. Later in life he had to start looking after himself as he didn't want to go through that again.

I first met Bri when I was about seventeen and started to venture in to town drinking in the Cosy Corner pub. Bri was a bouncer and without any doubt, one of the best at his job. He wasn't like your "typical bouncer" who would just come up, grab you and sometimes give you a sly hit on the side of your head. If ourselves or any other group started to get out of hand, Bri would just walk up, tap you on the back and say, "come on lads calm down" and that was enough, as people respected him.

About forty years ago I was in a pub called the Sturgeon, sitting with my sons' mother, when a dart was thrown and landed in between the two of us. I picked it up, went over to the owner of the dart and handed it back to him, he was told "these are for dartboards and not to be thrown at people." I turned my back on the culprit, and he tried a cheap shot from behind. I turned around swiftly and hit the guy with two hits, first one knocked him out, second one was for good measure and that was a well-known hard-nut whose name I can't reveal.

"Brian Sutherland was the calmest doorman I ever knew." - **Eddie Copland**

I was sitting in the Drift Inn speaking to Val Hutcheon, when a Glaswegian came across to our company. He started kicking me under the table, I told him to stop doing it. He threatened me, so I knocked him over the little partition, jumped over and he was out cold, so I either slapped or punched him just to make sure.

I left there, went up to the Clipper and my first words were "who's the hardest cunt in here?"

A certain tough-nut said, "me" so, I knocked him over two tables. As I was walking out the Clipper, police were on their way in, the Copper asked, "where's the trouble,"

"inside" I said and walked out calmly back to the Drift Inn.

I was on duty at Laffalots on a Thursday night, just myself. This Guy came in, all 6ft 4in and 'just as fucking wide,' he approached me and asked if I knew how he could get a job on the door, I explained it was best if someone knew you.

He replied "what if I took your job" then he walked away. Well, I was watching this guy and he beckoned me over, so who was I to refuse. I went over, and he said, "I'm going to create damage." *hmm!!* well two swift hits and he was on the deck! I Booted him a couple of times, dragged him over to a corner and smacked him a couple of times. I then took him into the toilet washed him up, spoke with him and found out he was in the army. I then kindly asked him to leave the premises.

As he was walking up the Shiprow he shouted back at me that he would be back, I replied, "you better take a Garrison with you then," I made a gesture to run after him, the cunt took off like a Gazelle being hunted by a Lion.

Ah, another classic was in Jimmy Wilson's on Hadden Street, a certain person was bullying a smaller guy. I went over to the person and told him to pick on someone his own size. He looked bewildered, I went to the toilet, came back, and joined the company I was with. I looked over and this guy was still bullying the small guy, so I went over and said to him "I will give you one free hit and then am going to bash you." He never took me up on the hit, so I headbutted him and he landed about two feet in the air. I sprang over to where he was lying and thumped him a couple of times again, just to make sure he understood why he was getting thumped.

It was Hogmanay and I was at Big Ali's pub in Tenerife, I went outside for a bit of fresh air and low and behold a guy was lying on the deck with some very severe bruising, I went back to the pub with him and spoke to Big Al.

It was now eleven in the morning and we had decided it was time to leave the pub. This Glaswegian boy was making his way towards me when Al and my partner at the time intervened. I was taken away to sit on a wall by Als' wife and his two sons. I must have sat there all of five minutes when one of the sons said "Ma just let Brian sort him out" I went and approached the ''Weegie loud mouth fucker'', hit him a cracker and he landed on his back. I was on top of him like Flash Gordon and pounded on him like there was no tomorrow. My hands were covered in his blood and to top it off, I pulled him up towards me and asked if he had enough. Not sure if the nod of his head said no, so gave him a few more to make sure until there was no movement, must admit I thought I had killed him.

I was working as a barman/door steward in a place called Willie Millers when, a party of three came into the bar. The tough nut told the Manager and Assistant Manager that he was going to go behind the bar to help himself. *Hmm* I said, "you're not,"

He retorted "pot calling kettle black," so I came from behind the bar and confronted him. He attempted to throw a punch but was slow, so the old faithful one, two, done the trick. He was on the ground very dazed indeed, I went to put my hands around his 'Fucking Fat neck' to choke the Cunt but was interrupted by a hook coming in from the side that connected right in the eye, I looked up at the person that done it, he apologised and said he meant it for the tough nut.

I had just come from an all-night party at a skipper's house in Garthdee with a friend of mine who was gay, he was a trawl fisherman. We got off the bus and went into the Schooner. My friend went to get us a drink and I heard these two guys, (one was English) saying, "hey! get us two pints as well you bender," *hmm!* I went over and laid both them out. HATE Fucking Bullies. FACT!

That same incident created a knock-on effect. I was behind the bar again when the owner told me to go on the door as someone had just came in with a hammer and threatened someone. I was standing on the door and I noticed a van stop further up the road and a group getting out. I walked up to the other exit and this 'plonker' came through the door, I explained that he was not getting in, he retorted "get tae fuck out the road monkey"

'Well' I turned my back as though I was going to walk away but came up with my elbow that landed on his jaw. I took him by the scruff of the jumper and marched his head towards the bandit which he kept banging into. I chucked the fucker out the door and went back inside to see how the rest of the lads were doing. Another satisfying day on the doors.

My arrest for the so-called glassing of the Flannie's incident was humorous. I had eluded the police most of the weekend and was in the Broadsword bar with some of the lads. We then decided to go back to my mate Puddings for a game of cards, 'well' eventually there was a knock on the door. I automatically went in to the bedroom and hid in the wardrobe, *hmm!* bad mistake the cunts had the warrant to search the place, correct! they found me in the wardrobe.

I went to court the next day on petition seven day lie down. Back up to court the following week and was remanded in custody until the trial, which was a sheriff and jury trial. Well I impeached J.R. However, the jury did not believe this during the trial, so I was found guilty of assault but was fortunate that the jury decided that the glasses on the table had caused the injury when I smashed his head down on the table and not my doing. How lucky was sixteen months, and my three months lie down was taken into consideration for the offence.

When I was doing my time for an assault, I was doing my sentence along with McG and others, I got into a fight that set something else in motion.

I was sitting at a table of four playing a card game called 'Bella.' Now and again I would drop a card and a hand would hit me on the head, *hmm! I* told the cunt to stop it and he laughed.

Next day same thing happened well needless to say I was up like a flash and smashed the cunt a few times, the screws came in and pulled me off. Next, we were being escorted to our cells, the cunt in front turned around and used a motion that I was going to get my throat cut! Well, as he was heading towards his cell, I broke free from the Screws and started chasing the cunt along the corridor, the bastard closed his cell door and opened his spy hole. I told him, "any fucking time and I will take the knife from you and reverse the situation." Screws caught up and escorted me back to my cell. We were both up in front of the Governor and lost fourteen days remission.

Think it was the next day, I was walking past the Cobblers Shop when I saw a Con I knew, he was doing ten years and the guy he was helping lift a table was doing eight years, as the guy doing ten years was a powerlifter, I said, "thought you would be lifting that yourself." The guy then came up to my cell and hit me with a pole from the scaffolding erected outside my cell, so I knocked the shit out of him and a few screws as well.

As I was going down the stairs, standing there on the second landing was the upstart Kansas Kelly, as I was passing him I said "you're not good enough either" so, I lost another fourteen days for that.

I had only twelve days left of my sentence remaining, so I wrote to the Secretary of State asking for my remission to be reduced. Anyway, rumour had it I was going to be released on the Monday *hmmmm!*

Sunday afternoon I was showering when a person, (who is now dead) came into the shower. This guy was moved from Peterhead prison for using people as pin cushions, anyway I saw him with a towel wrapped

24

around his hand and thought '*who is he,*' found out soon enough, I bent down to pick up the soap and Wow! the shower door was booted open. A home-made shank was stuck into my back and into my head, as I was moving towards him I managed to grab his arms and push them into his own body, however he managed to catch me at the side of the eye. I fucking head butted him across the shower room and was about to go tackle him when two screws entered the shower area.

The double lifer turned towards the screws and as he walked towards them they walked backwards. I then turned to look at my back and realised there was a hole in it, so I put a towel around it to stop the bleeding. As I was walking to the surgery I was going past the 'Can' also known as the 'toilets' *ah!* Now, Kansas Kelly, the two screws and the double lifer were all standing inside the Can. I told Kansas Kelly he's still not good enough! And, just so you get the full picture, this man was a category A prisoner that always had to be escorted and always and to shower alone *hmmm!*

This happened at two in the afternoon and they told my mum at eleven thirty that night.

I collapsed at the prison surgery and woke up in the prison van going to the hospital. I lost consciousness again, next thing I woke up with a tube in my lung and the two screws told me that I had been released from prison.

"*To say fighting was meant for me.... I would say many of us that can take care of ourselves we did not intend it to be who we are it just happened that way.*"
-**Brian Sutherland**

JOE GILL

*"I remember Joe Gill who was younger than me,
about in his 20's – 30's. He had just won his fight in
the first two minutes at the booth and then shouted
out that he would take on any two at a time. These
two gypsies stepped up and took him to his word.
Well, as you have guessed Joe knocked them both out
in the first round, and in my opinion was one of the
hardest guys I have ever saw."*
- Dod Moore

One day when Joe was at the Castlegate, he noticed a photographer and his pet monkey. The guy was treating the monkey bad, so Joe went over and had a few words with him. Joe took the monkey off him, and then took it home to his house. When he let it loose it chased George all over the house. He then took it over to his mother and fathers house on Polworth Road. His father was in the back bedroom 'Bleezin drunk' having a sleep, so Joe put the monkey in the bed beside his father.

Well, you can imagine his face when he woke up in bed with a monkey lying next to him. After a while the police arrived to take the monkey back to its owner, I think Joe should have been a vet or something as another time he ended up stealing two horses.

There was this guy who used to hang about with Joe, he was a bit of a "fearty", the things they use to do to him like hanging a washer on a bit of string above his bedroom window so when the wind blew it would tap on his window. The poor man would be lying in his bed terrified and scared to move.

The guy got his own back one day when he was sitting watching Joe and Billy wallpapering, they hung the wallpaper upside down and he didn't bother to tell them until they had finished.

"He was very proud of his kid's, grandkids and great-grandkids. You couldn't go and see him without him saying this one did this and this one did that. He was so funny with his stories I could have listened to him all night. When me and my husband Paul who is English used to visit him, he used to shout, "come in Jake and take that English cunt in with you." We used to laugh for ages after visiting him."
- Jackie Dabell

"I'm glad to be in the family as Joe was a legend and will never be forgotten for he was one hard-nut in his day and his memory will live forever."
- Hazel Lamont

"Most of his stories was funny about back in his days when they got up to some mischief and it wasn't all about scrapping" **- Jim Moore**

My Grandad, Joe didn't have much left on his knuckles with all the boxing and street fighting in his days. When I was a bairn I asked him, what happened to his hands. Well, he told me that he got captured from the Japs in the war and they tortured him and cut his knuckles out, and the Japs called him Jungle Joe. I was so impressed and proud of him I couldn't wait to get into school the next day to tell my teachers, they must have thought I had some imagination plus the fact, I don't think he got as far as Stonehaven during the war – in fact, I think they were still trawling at that time. - **Jim Moore**

"Joe was a gentleman through and through"
- Angela Lennox

Joe was brought up in the Castlegate. Joe and Gordon Westland used to go around the boxing booths when they were young to earn extra cash, Sunny Ogg used to pal about with him as well. One day they had a big card game going on, so Joe fixed it for Ted Crook to switch off the power when he gave him a nod. Well, power went off and when it went back on all the kitty money had gone .

Joe had three children Liz, Kate, and young Joe.

DICK GRIBBLE

Dick was in the army for three and a half years and was going to sign up again when his wife Frannie got pregnant, but he decided to stay home and look after his family. Dick was also posted on two occasions to Northern Ireland, He told me a few amazing stories about his time over there.

At the Waterton club having a good time and something happened over at the bar, I went over, and my brother Roberts mate was fighting with some folk. I noticed Robert was away to jump in so I pulled him aside and said, "you just keep out of this" I then calmed everything down and told everyone to get back to their seats and told the other lot to fuck off back to their seats. They were sitting about three tables behind us.

After a while they started pinging the pull wraps off the cans at us, so one of our crowd shouted over to them, "you ping any more of that things at us and we are coming over there to smash your fucking faces in!" Next thing, they ping another one at us, well, that was enough! a huge fight started.

I was giving it shit and knocking them everywhere, never seen anything like that, everyone in the whole place was fighting, it was like something out of a western. Next thing I heard my mate Babbie shouting, "Dick, Dick!" as I looked over this fucker had him by the neck and was trying to choke him. I said, "Babbie move your head to one side," as he did, I knocked this guy for six, as we looked around every single person was fighting with each other. Babbie burst out laughing and said, "Dick look over there!". I looked over and the only person not fighting was Billy Duguid, as he was going around drinking everyone's drink. Next thing, the police arrived and we were all put on our bus. We were all having a laugh and a drink on the bus and heading into the town for more drink.

We reached Woodside, so I said to stop the bus so we can all go into the chip shop for something to eat, next thing, one of the guys on the bus walked over and tried to smash my mate on the face with the heel of his shoe. I grabbed him and knocked him flying! Well, it all kicked off again, on the bus I was going crazy, I was jumping over seats shouting, "I'm going to fucking kill them!" the bus slammed on its brakes, we were all still fighting, when it all calmed down the bus started moving again. I looked over and it was my mate driving, unknown to me the driver fucked off and left his bus while we were all kicking off.

We stopped at the statue on Union Terrace and there were cops everywhere waiting for us. We got off the bus and we all started fighting again. The cops were just grabbing anyone and throwing them into the van, a few of us walked away up the town and decided to go to the Palace or the Pally night club but we were all dying for a piss! So, we went back to Union Terrace, my mates Babbie and Billy Duguid were walking away behind us, and as we were walking down a bunch of guys walked past us. We looked around and the next thing, Babbie and Billy were fighting with them, we ran up and sorted the guys out and then started to walk down Bridge Street to go to the Palace night club. next thing, Billy was fighting with this guy. A few of us just carried on towards the Palace as there were a few who stayed back with Billy.

A while passed by and in walked the rest of the guys I was saying, "where the fuck have you lot been? and where's Billy?"

they said, "oh he is away to hospital." I was going nuts with them saying "you fucking let him get a doing in?"

they said "No Billy had a hold of the guy and when he went to hit him the guy ducked, and Billy crashed his hand off the Granite, Robert the Bruce statue and broke his hand."

Another time, Billy and his wife who I was drinking all day with left the pub to go home, about twenty minutes later this guy ran into the pub and said Billy had been rushed to hospital.

I said, "he can't be as he just left."

Found out that when he got to his door he had lost his door keys, he then decided to climb up the drainpipe to his top floor flat, (remember he was pissed) he managed to get all the way to the top and grabbed hold of the railing to pull himself in. Just as he did his cat who was called 'LUCKY' jumped out on him, he shit himself! and fell clean off the drainpipe.

I went into hospital to see him and he said to me "Dick the funniest thing about it was, as I was falling past these windows everyone was watching different TV channels."

The day of the Piper Alpha tragedy, we were all in Willie Millers pub and a few of the boys nipped next door to the Cosy Corner pub, my brother Bob left just after them.

About an hour later my cousin Jessie ran in screaming "quick your mates are getting attacked in the Cosy Corner." I was thinking *fuck my brother Bob's there,* so myself and about four others ran around to the Cosy Corner and as we got there, my brother Bob had this bouncer by the hair grabbing him down the stairs. I ran up the stairs to help my other mates, looked around and no one was there. Ran back down, looked around the corner and seen this huge crowd of people and the police holding them all back, noticed one of my mates and asked, what was going on? He was screaming "Oh! Oh! the boys going to die", there was a pool of blood everywhere, someone had put his arm through the window. Someone then shouted to say it was one of our mates.

I was charging through the crowd and pushing the police away, next thing this BIG! Fucking Police Sergeant grabbed me. I was screaming at him to let me go as it was my mate that was bleeding, Babbie was also screaming at him.

The copper says, "Its OK son, the ambulance is on its way,"

Babbie said, "It's not him I'm worried about, the cunt has got on my new £150 jacket"

The first fight I can remember was when I was about eight years old and these two men hit my brother and called me a little bastard. I was thinking *no one calls me a bastard as I know my mother and father.* I picked up a stick to hit him but ended up throwing it away and just ran over and started kicking his legs. Next thing someone shouts "Dick here's your father coming down", this guy turned to me and said "Oh! so this is your father," I ran over to my dad and said, "Da that two men just hit Robert and called me a bastard,"

My da said "is that right!" he then approached these two big guys and remember, my father was just a little guy. He took off his jacket, handed it to Robert and rolled up his sleeves. I was thinking *oh my god my father is going to get killed,* so I looked around me for an iron bar to go and help him, next thing my father goes Bang! Bang! and the two of them hit the deck like a ton of bricks. That was the only time I ever saw my Da lift his hand.

I have always been able to take care of myself and most of my situations were helping other people.

I was on guard duty one day, and at that time we had to search everyone that had passed the point. This guy squeezed past me, his jacket opened and I noticed he had a gun in its holster over his shoulder. I shouted over to my mate Taffy "This fuckers got a gun!" the guy took off , I ran after him but I didn't realise I chased him into a 'no-go' area, as soldiers weren't allowed to go into that area. I was tearing after him and next thing crowds of people were blocking my way calling me everything, so I decided to walk back. I didn't run back as to show that lot I wasn't scared of them. I got back and about twenty minutes later the RSM came up to me and said, "Jock, the Commander wants to see you," I was worried because the only time he wanted to see you, was if there was something wrong at home.

In his office, standing to attention he says, "Jock I'm putting you on a charge."

I said, "what for Sir?"

he said, "you were chasing a guy into a no-go area and he has reported you for swearing at him," What? the same guy who was wearing a gun? I couldn't believe it, I got locked up for a night and ended up fighting with the Military Police.

I used to box in the army until this guy put the head on me in the ring, I ended up kicking him in the balls and got torn into him! I threw the referee out of the way and got disqualified. That was my boxing days over. I got put in the cookhouse for a week because the RSM lost money on me on the fight.

Just out of the army and I got myself a job as a bouncer in the Douglas. One afternoon we were sitting in the pub and one of the guys said, "we can't find Terrance" we then got a phone call to say he was in the hospital because he got a doing in, from the bouncers at the Douglas Hotel. Anyway, I got to the bottom of the story. Terrance was walking by the dance-floor on his way to the toilet smoking his cig, bouncers approached him and said, "you shouldn't be on the dance-floor with your cig,"

Terrance said, "I'm not dancing, I'm on my way to the toilet," next thing the bouncer grabbed him, pulled him out into the back doors, took him outside and started laying fuck out of him along with the rest of the bouncers. About fourteen of us went up to the hospital to see Terrance, we didn't recognise him because of the mess they made of him.

I Bumped into a guy called Rusty that played in the band in the Douglas, I asked him about what happened that night. He told me the bouncers were out of order and picked on Terrance for no reason. We waited until he got out of the hospital to find out the whole story from him.

I went back to see Rusty to tell him to let the bouncers know we were coming to get them! At that time the Douglas had about twenty bouncers on as they had upstairs, downstairs and the hotel. "Tell them we will wait until closing time when everyone has gone"

Rusty got back to me and said, "they will be waiting for you anytime and to bring it on."

About eight of us walked in and right away I spotted the bouncer who started everything, shouted over to him, "Hey Arsehole, when this club is empty you and your bouncer mates are getting kicked to fuck!" he just sniggered back at me and I was about to attack him there and then, but the boys held me back and said, "no leave it until everyone has gone and let the fucker sweat." I was sitting at a table and the head bouncer who I knew very well came over to speak to me about I, my words to him were "John, we are going to do the lot of them in, I like you, so if you are standing with him you will get it as well,"

He said, "Dick, I wasn't on that night when your mate got a laying on." He walked over to all the bouncers and said, "do you lot know what you have got yourselves into, as I know that boys very very well and you don't want to be fucking about with them."

Most of the bouncers left and there were only about eight bouncers left, so I challenged the main bouncer and as he walked over one hit and he was out cold! I went over to the bar and told the others "we will be back next week to sort the rest of you lot out." The manager came over and said, "Excuse me, sir can I have a word"

My reply was "FUCK OFF! and are you going to try to throw us out?" to my amazement he said "NO! NO! but would you and your friends like to take over as bouncers for my club?" We ended up working there for over three years and hardly any trouble, if there was any, we used to take the guys up the lane outside and let them fight each other in a fair manner, and after their fight…. let them back in and that was the end of it.

Funny story about Dick and his wife Franny. Dick was married to Franny for ages, but his family had never met or seen her. One day Dick was on the doors at the Douglas, and Franny went there for the night. She was away to sit down at a table with Dicks family and they turned around to her and said "Oh sorry you can't sit here as it's reserved for family"
Franny said, "I am family, I'm Dicks wife"
Well, they shouted, "Dick you cunt! you told us Franny was fat, ugly, had glasses and a snotty nose."
Dick said if he never married Franny he would probably have spent most of his days in prison.

I was about six or seven, I remember the police would never come into Kilgour as they were too scared to.

I also remember the time there was a riot at the Broadsword when the police cars got turned over and set on fire and the police were running all over Tillydrone just to get away from everyone.

The hard guys, when I was a kid, were Harry Daniels, Kenny McGuire, Jimmy Mason, and the Stewart's.

When I was about fourteen years old these two coppers, (one had a huge fucking nose) caught me smoking and shouted "you, you little bastard get over here."
so, I walked over and said to him "who are you calling a bastard?"
he said "I wouldn't mind giving you a thumping"
"you couldn't knock stew off a bap, you big nose fucker," then I said to him "I can't hear what you are saying because you are away up there

and I'm only little and down here," so, as he bent down I put the head on him an ran off, he was shouting "wait till I get my hands on you, you little bastard!"

I started playing football at the Lad's Club and going to the club disco, "back in the days" the boys would never go up dancing with the girls, but not me I was up on the floor giving it a bit of this and that. I remember a song that was out at the time called, 'Johnny Reggae here comes Johnny Reggae', and when I used to walk in, the girls would start singing 'Richard, Richard Gribble here comes Richard Gribble, Richard Gribble lay on me.'

One night after the disco I headed home down the hill under the bridge, which at that time was called Lovers Bridge, now it's called Muggers Bridge. Walking up my path and I heard these voices, it was older men's voices, so I crept in, and out popped these two coppers with their Batman cloak on, they used to wear when it was raining. I said "Fuck you" I ran off and they couldn't catch me. Every night for years I was dreading walking up my path, so I started to sing and whistle.

As I was walking I kept listening because they were always waiting for me. After a while when I got home, just before I went up the path I would shout up "Hey Da, could you put the lobby light on?" because I knew the coppers wouldn't touch me with the light on. This went on for years and every time the light went on they would fuck off, so the second time I shouted up to my Da to put the light on he shouts, "why do you keep wanting me to put the lights on,"

I said I was scared of the dark because I didn't want him to find out what I did.

A few years later I said to my Da, "Do you want to know the reason I keep shouting up to you to put on the lights when I get home."

His reply was "yes son because you're scared of the dark."

So that night I was away out again, I told him I wouldn't shout up and just to sneak halfway down the landing and not to put the light on, I would be home at eleven pm, and that he would see what would happen.

At eleven o'clock, I walked into the lobby and knowing my father was watching, I heard the voices. "Here comes this little bastard and he hasn't shouted up to his Da,"

I ran towards them and shouted, "come on then you dirty bastards!" the four of them ran towards me, my father jumped down the stairs and they ran out the back door and jumped over the fence just to get away. My father ran after them shouting, "Come back you cowards and he will fight you one at a time, you are not men and not policemen!" That's when my dad suggested I join the army as that cops would have it in for me.

Three years later, my first day out of the army and my mate took me down to Froghall. We were having a drink and my mate got a phone call to say something was going on at his house. So, off we went in a taxi. We got there, and my mate ran up the stairs, next thing he had this guy hanging out the window. I ran up to calm things down, next thing the coppers turned up Just at the point my mate picked up a fire poker and went to hit the guy over the head with it, but just in time, I grabbed it from him. There were a few coppers in the house, they pointed at me and asked if I had anything to do with it, everyone said "no he was calming everything down," I started walking down the stairs, and running up were more coppers, they said, "where the fuck are you going?" I noticed right away it was that Big Fucking nose copper from years back, anyway the cops that was in the house said "No its nothing to do with him just let him past," as I walked past them he hit me over the head with his baton again. That was enough so I went for him and did him in, his mate ran down so I did him in as-well and every other cop that came running to me, next thing it was the C.I.D and I did them as-well.

I got out the building and they grabbed my brother, I told them "Fucking leave my brother as it's nothing to do with him," they started knocking the fuck out of me with their batons. I was going crazy and giving them as good back. Bob turned to the coppers and said, "leave him because he won't stop till you stop," they stopped, so I calmed down. They handcuffed me and the next thing another baton over my head then they marched me outside. This guy ran and tried kicking me in the balls with four policemen looking on, they didn't do anything, I said, "what you going to do about that then?"

Their reply was "you deserved it," Now I was like an animal. I knocked them over, started kicking fuck out of them and still in handcuffs. Someone shouted get the police dog on him. Next thing, this dog took some bite out of my arse and I've still got the scar now. Well, I bent over and sunk my teeth into the dog and took a chunk out of it, the dog ran up beside Spencer's paint factory with the copper screaming, "Oh my dog! My dog! What have you done to my dog?"

Most people would have heard this story as it was a big story in Aberdeen when it happened.

Dick got a phone call from a friend (who was running a well-known pub at the time) three guys walked in with a shotgun, threatened his friend, and told him they would be back to shoot him later. Dick went to the pub, him and his friend were sitting in the pub in the dark waiting for them to come back. A knock on the door and Dick looked out and noticed it was them back again. Dick looked through the letter box to see them and couldn't believe his eyes, as it turned out it was old friends of his, he told them not even think about it.

One day Dick got a phone call from two of his brother's mates,

who were out in a club in the outskirts of Aberdeen. They were asking him to come out as soon as, because they were going to get attacked from someone. Dick got out there right away and walked into the pub. He looked around, his two brothers mates over at one side and on the other side, a table full of guys and some guy on his own standing at the bar.

Dick asked no questions and walked up to the table full of guys, he started knocking the shit out of them all, after he finished with them he went over to his brother's mates who were looking very shocked at what had just happened. Dick said, "what the fuck is up with your faces?"

They said "Dick, you got the wrong guys, the guy that was starting with us is that guy standing at the bar on his own."

Dick went back up to the group he just attacked and said, "guys I'm sorry, could you do me a favour and go over and kick the shit out of that two guys over there?" pointing at his brothers mates. LOL

"Dick Gribble, got to be one of the nicest guy you will ever meet. A true gentleman and total old school, definitely one in a million"
- **Scott Allan**

"BRILLIANT GUY"- **Jeanette Middleton**

"Known Dick for years he is a Toff."
- **Richard Turner**

"My Dad, he is old fashioned I swore in the house and got my mouth washed with soap, gadz! he just says it like it is & it's pretty scary fan he's pissed off everyone vacates the house ha-ha xx love him to bits though" xxx
*- **Lisa Gribble***

STEVE MOORE

Steve was born in Torry but brought up in Woodside. He then moved back to Torry for secondary school. At Sixteen years old he joined the Gordon Highlanders.

Back in 1991 I was twenty-two years old and still in the army which I had been in since I left school. I was just home from an active tour in Northern Ireland, so I was ultra-fit and strong. I have always been naturally strong for my size, I was only thirteen stone opposed to the "fat cunt" I am today at nineteen stone. Anyway, I had already been in many of fights through my army days and also when home on leave with many a doorman, partly or mostly because I was Dod Moore's son and because of the reputation he had when he was a handful in the town, the Mooring etc., I was finding I was getting a bit of a rep myself not what I wanted in life it just happened that way.

I must say I have never been a bully and never picked on anyone or started on anyone for no reason, that's why to this day I have no real enemies.

One night I was out in town with my good mate Davie Ogston and a few others. At the end of the night we were at our usual kebab shop on Bridge Street getting a pizza kebab from my good pal Sied, or also known as Vito. We were in waiting for food chatting up this couple of birds and having a laugh when in came these three guys, biggest cunts I

43

had ever seen in my life! I mean they were huge! they had short military type hair and one had a Mohican he honestly looked like B.A. Baracus, they were all Americans and loud as fuck! they ended up sitting behind us banging on the tables and harassing everyone that passed them. They asked this big guy who was in the queue if he wanted an arm wrestle, the guy said, "no" but they kept on at him so, he eventually did but he got hammered!

The Yanks started shouting "Any other mortals fancy a lesson in pure strength?" all the birds and Davie were looking at me, so I had to, I couldn't help myself. I turned to the guy and said, "I'll play you mate but look at the size of you, you're massive! I'm just little you'll have to give me a chance," ha!

His mate turned and said to me "Beat it you puny little cunt or I'll step on your face,"

I said, "yeah why don't you arm wrestle me then see how tough you are."

'hahaha'. he laughed and said he wouldn't waste his time,

I said, "we'll make it worth your while, put £50 on it." ha! they liked that and sprung to attention. I said, "let's go." We put the money down and went for it, everyone was cheering for me 'obviously' all from Aberdeen, they just wanted me to shut the loud mouths up, within a seconds, I knew this guy was no match for me but I wasn't going to show them that. I struggled to make them think I couldn't win so I could get £50 off the next guy. I beat him, then played the second one. Again, the fool had no strength I took a bit longer to beat this one, but I only had one more to go...the main dude, the B.A. Baracus guy.

I winked to my mate and said, "I've got this." Before I arm wrestled the cunt I said to him, "Ok me and you pal, what about we double the money to £100," he just laughed in my face and said, "no problem I'm going to crush you."

I put the £100 down that I had already won and just before we were about to start I said to him, "I'll tell you what I'll do mate, since judging by your mates strengths, you're from America and I'm far stronger because I'm from Scotland. How about I just put you down in three seconds flat and If I can't put you down in three seconds flat then you win and take the money,"

He laughed and replied, "I have never been beat, never mind being put down in three seconds."

I said, "no problem let's go, someone count to three,"

A bird that was standing watching shouted "one...."

Then I put the guy down in a second, he was going mental saying he wasn't ready. He was just a fanny, so I said, "Ok, let's go again I'll give you a second chance, you say go and the lassie will count,"

"Ok" he says, "GO!", same thing again, down he went in a second, I took the £100 turned to them and said, "Don't take it to heart guys It's just that Scottish are naturally strong, and Americans are full of hot air."

They were raging as everyone was cheering me on and you could see it in their faces they were humiliated, just then I got my pizza and left with my mates. Davie said, "I know you'd beat them I'm surprised they never kicked off though as you made a total cunt of them."

We were eating our pizza walking up Bridge street, when we turned right at the top of the road where the old C & A used to be, all of a sudden, the three guys came running around the corner. They shouted on us, so we stopped and looked around. The guys were walking towards us saying, "It's payback time but, this time it's going to be with clenched fists," my mate Davie is not the fighting type, so I gave him my pizza to hold.

The fools just walked in a line straight into it, 'Right Hook' clean on the sweet spot! 'Left Hook' again right on the jaw! ;Mohican guy' ripped off his shirt. He was huge, he had bigger tits than Jordan! he came running towards me so, I stepped to the side and BANG! right hook and the same outcome, out cold.

The three of them lying unconscious, another mate of mine from school, Lee O'Conner walked past and said, "Fuck sake Moore, Rocky Balboa eat your heart out." Job done! just three bams bullying folk because of their size. Anyway, I got my pizza back and started walking down the road, we looked back and the three of them were still lying there, then, I heard the sirens coming. I was thinking, *they had to be for me*, so I ran back along Union Street, down Bridge Street toward the old railway across from the Tivoli bingo, with the coppers hot on my heals.

They had already arrested my pal Dave and was quizzing him, but he was saying nothing. The three guys were in an ambulance still out cold Davie heard over the radio in the police car *'yeah we've caught him, half way up a lamp post on Poinernook Road.'* ha-ha! that's true! I was sick of running, the coppers were away to catch me, so I stopped at a lamp post and tried to get up the railway line above the arches, but halfway up there was barbed wire and thick grease, I was Fucked! the coppers just stood there until I fell off and straight into handcuffs.

I was taken back up to Union street beside C&A, Davie in one car and me in another. Two of the guys had woke up and they came to the car to identify me as the one who knocked them out. Give the three guys their due, they said it was all their fault, the guy came over and said, "respect man" as he'd never been knocked out like that before. They didn't want to press charges, so they were left to walk away broken men, ha!

My pizza was freezing and I was starving with all the running so I went back to 'Vito's' to get another one, I was telling him what just happened, he laughed like fuck and gave me my pizza free ha! Brilliant. I was a hero for at least one night and no one was really hurt just their pride ha-ha!

"I ran a site in Aberdeen and was forever getting robbed at night. tools, materials, etc., Steve said I will go in at nights as your security guard and sort it out. From the first to his last day there nothing ever went missing again, although he did get a bit upset because someone shit in his kettle."

- Ian Esslemont

THE TURNERS

Ricky moved up to Aberdeen when he was in his twenties. He stayed in Ferrier's for a while and then moved up to Northfield.

The first time I ever met Ricky was when he started to come into the Byron with Bopter and Jim Robertson. After a couple of times talking to him and getting to know him, I realised what a toff of a guy he was and never ever, saw him loose his rag or raise his voice, but we knew not to get on the wrong side of him. At that time there used to be about twenty of us that sat in the corner and every time Ricky came in he would always come over to us and ask how we were keeping and if we were staying out of trouble.

The last time I saw Ricky was when we walked into the Lorne bar we ended up sitting with him the rest of the night having a good drink and a good laugh. It was about a year later I found out that he had passed away.

"One day we were standing at the bar myself, Ricky and a few others. Over comes this guy, he was starting to piss us all off. I'm jumping about and was ready to rip this fuckers' head off until Ricky turns around and said to me Jim calm down because you don't want to be rolling about the floor with this idiot, there are better ways to deal with situations like this.

This fucker is now standing behind me, so Ricky sticks his arm out and moves me to one side and next thing a fist comes flying past me and catches this fucker straight on the chin and knocks him clean out. Ricky turns to me and said now lad that's the way to do it. I was a good bit younger than Ricky and Bopter but learned so much off them."
- Jim Robertson

Ricky Turner

KEV TURNER

On a Saturday me and my family would stay in and have a 'chipper' supper. One day my Ma went down to Doug's chipper van which used to park outside the Dancing Cairns pub, when she came back her face was chalk white and we all said, "what's up with you ma?'

My ma just said, "nothing's wrong with me I'm fine," but when we got through to the kitchen she said, "someone down at Doug's chipper threatened me!"

I was only about ten years old at the time. Me, my brothers, and my dad all headed down to Doug's chipper van, my da headed straight into the Dancing Cairns to find the guy, and next thing he came out with the guy by the scruff of the neck, my Da stood aside and said "Ok boys get in about him," my Da was standing there while me and my brother's argued who was going to batter him, so I just ran over and pushed the guy to the ground and got stuck into him. The guy never fought back because he knew if he did my father would have Killed him!

I was about 15 when I was sent to approve school. My first one was Oakbank, they said, "there's nothing we can do for this kid." They then moved me to Brimmond, I had loads of fights in there.

I always pushed and pushed my way to the front as I never wanted to be left at the back.

Next move was to Polmont where I was always fighting with these Glaswegian's and sticking up for the Aberdonian's.

It was getting embarrassing watching the way they were being treated by these 'weegies.' They weren't fighting back and sticking up for themselves, because at that time a lot of the guys were sent down there for drug addiction, not me, I had never touched a drug and was more alert than most of them.

I felt sorry for the Aberdeen guys because every other week they were getting bullied or slashed, so I drummed it into their heads 'boys you have to start fighting back and getting into this lot, ok! you might not win but you never know, you might win, and at the end of the day you're getting bullied anyway, so you have nothing to lose!'

After about two years in there the Glasgow mob backed away from the Aberdeen lads and then they started picking on the Dundee lads. at that time, I started getting a bit of a name for myself. When I got out I started doing a lot of favours for people, battering this one and the next one and getting a bit of a reputation.

When I was in young offenders there was this top Glaswegian called Gemmell who was running the place. One day I was sitting eating my dinner and some fucker threw a tomato off the back of my head, I turned around and there were about twenty Glaswegian's standing there and I said, "who did that?" they all just put their heads down, and not one of them said a word.

I went up the stairs and up came Gemmell, he said, "Turner do you think you're a big man? and do you think because you're from Aberdeen you're going to run this place?"

I replied "NO, I don't think that," I then said to him "ok come into my cell and sort it out!"

Gemmell replied "Oh no we don't have to sort it out, "and he left it at that.

Two days later this little shit came up and tried to stab me, but I ended up kicking him all over the place. Later, Gemmell came up and again said, "Ok but don't think you can run this place." It was

Gemmell's way of backing down from me because he knew I wasn't going to back down from No One.

This guy phoned me and asked for help, as some other guy was threating him and said he would murder his mother. I went with him to the boys' house and kicked the door in. Next thing this dog came towards me, so I punched it straight in the face and the dog went flying! Went into the bedroom to get the guy and started to knock the fuck out of him! I looked over and noticed this dartboard on the wall with darts sticking into it, so I said to my mate "Watch this," I took the darts out of the board and started to stick them in the guy's arse as he was lying on the floor.

Probably the toughest fight I ever had was with my old pal Scott Montgomery because we were both drunk at the time. He reminded me of Bopter, same height and build.

The first time Amber set eyes on Kev was in the Hen House pub in town and yes, you have guessed it, Kev was knocking the shit out of someone at the time.

Kev admits if it wasn't for his Amber and his kids he would probably be doing a long or a life sentence in jail.

I have a scar down my arm and the story to that is... I was drinking in town and we were invited to this party down at King Street. We pulled up in a taxi and went into the house. I was getting a bit rowdy, and this couple of guys jumped on me.

I grabbed one by the throat until he passed out while the other one was still punching me. Now I'm outside and thinking *did I just get beat there!*

I was shouting, "I'm not having this!" so, I noticed this tree and tried to pull it out by the roots to smash through their window, but I wasn't strong enough to get it out.

I walked over to the window and put my hand through it and as I went to pull it back it ripped my arm open. The blood was everywhere, and I was thinking *SHIT! what have I just done!* It was bleeding so badly.

I said to my mate, "Take off your shoe laces and tie it around my arm to stop the blood flow."

Next thing police arrived followed by an ambulance. My mate phoned the wife and told her that I was in the hospital because I had cut my hand.

"I rushed up to the hospital, walked up to the receptionist and told her my name, she said, "oh sit down, sit-down," next, someone came over with this form and took me to the family room, (that's where they take you if it's very bad news).

53

*Next the surgeon walks in with this form, I was thinking the worst and I started to take a panic attack, he then asked me to sign this form as they were away to amputate his arm, but I refused point blank and said I'm not signing that as I knew Kev would have rather had an arm that wasn't functional rather than no arm at all. Twelve hours of surgery and thank god I didn't sign that form as they saved his arm." - **Amber Turner***

"Brilliant guy with no ego either."
*- **Fred Munroe***

*"I was up at a party in Rosemount, after a while and a few drinks we all decided to go into town, and because it was a lovely summer day Kev turned up with a pair of shorts and a t.shirt. We told him he was wasting his time going into town, because of the way he was dressed the bouncers wouldn't let him in. Kev was having none of it, so we got to the nightclub door and I couldn't believe it the bouncers just let him walk right into the club and let him do what he pleased as they knew not to get on the wrong side of him." - **Neil Bevy***

"Kev's brand new always has been"
*- **Cheryl Burt***

"A great hard-working lad, not a better family man, you could meet." - **Scott Booth**

I have known about this family for years but only ever spoke to Ricky the father, who was a toff. My son Lee was pals with his sons. Over the years, I have heard so much about Kev. After my interviews with most of the guys they all said the same, that Kev is one of the top guys in Aberdeen that no one wants to get on the wrong side of. After spending about four hours in his company Kev and his wife Amber were brilliant and a joy to speak to.

I have never met their mother May but on many occasions my friends "The Batty's" have said what a lovely woman she is, and this is backed up by everyone I talk to about May.

Richard and Mark, I have only spoke to on the group but seem very nice guys.

Ricky Turner

ALEX GIBSON

If my late husband Alex was here he could have told you a few stories about the Hard-Men and Market Street, the East Neuk bar Tillydrone and Torry.

Alex passed away three years ago and all I have is memories that he left me. Alex's best pal and sidekick was Sandy Gibson who had been hung, knifed a few times, and also burnt in a house fire. He even went back to the burned-out house that night just for a sleep.

Sandy's late girlfriend was Aggie McPherson which a few people didn't get on with, but she thought the world of me, I don't know why. Aggie even said to Alex "what the fuck is a nice lassie like Helen going out with a basket case like you?" Aggie was a proper hard-case and spent time in Cortonvale ladies prison.

I remember one day in a pub when she was going to take a water jug over Alex mates' head for telling her to shut the fuck up. I thought Aggie was great and wouldn't say a bad word against her. The last time I bumped into Sandy he told me to take care and started to cry, his last words were, "I so miss Aggie she might have been a Bam and a Hard-Nut, but she was my Hard-Nut." Sandy was classed as a Hard-Nut but deep down he was a pussycat, he and Aggie were the 'Bonnie and Clyde' of Aberdeen.

There was another time in the pub when this guy asked Alex's wife Helen up for a dance and as Alex looked over, the guy grabs Helen by the arse! Alex picked him up, threw him over the bar counter, smashed him up against the bar gantry and smashed all the spirits on the wall.

Alex was a fun-loving husband with a bad streak in him he did the wrong things for the right reasons. He didn't mess about when it came to fighting back in the days, one punch and he was king of the ring

Alex was brought up with nothing, he lived in the Attics in the Gallowgate on North-street before moving to Froghall. He was about ten before he saw a real bath. He moved there with his mother, father two brothers, and two sisters.

Times were very hard, he used to go down to the fish market with his father and pick up any fish that was lying around and take it up to the fish-shop downstairs where they lived, in return he would get two white puddings and chips to feed the family. He also had a paper round, but his wages went to his mother.

Alex was an altar boy which he got a half-crown for his singing along with a good friend of his Andy Lawson in St Machar Cathedral, again, he never seen a penny as it went to his family. Alex wasn't a greedy person he was brought up poor with nothing.

Xmas was the day he loved, especially in the kitchen as he loved seeing people eat and having fun, he even took his son Jamie's friend in when he had nowhere to go and fed him as he knew what it was like to have nothing. His speciality was his chicken fish cakes. People used to ask for his recipe but always told them they were made with a pinch of love.

Alex got barred from the Portland club for ninety-nine years for knocking out a club member. Alex used to laugh about it and say I don't know how I got barred as I wasn't even a member. He also got barred from the Butchers Arms pub in Inverurie as there was a huge brawl there and some guy lost an eye. Alex got barred for throwing a guy through the window.

Alex did a bit of time for his friend Sandy and was sent down for thirty days at the "Torry Hotel" for cashing someone's giro.

Sandy was a great football player and was going to sign for Man Utd, they even flew Sir Matt Busby up from Manchester to sign Sandy but sadly Sandy got time that day and was sent to Borstal.

One day in the Glens bar with little Ronnie, Bobby Cline and his fourteen-year-old son Jamie who was having a quiet game of pool. In walked this guy who was a woman beating cunt! and offered to play his son for £20. Well, Alex was just about to clobber him with the pool cue when his son said "No! da just leave him and I will take him on," so he played him and took the £20 off him, the guy just rushed out the pub without a word.

Alex did a lot of things he wasn't proud of, he took a lot of things to the grave with him, so he will be up there with half of the Aberdeen Hard -Nuts running a mock.

Alex was a loving husband. A loving grandad and a loving dad which we will sadly miss. R.I.P

NEIL
(RAMBO)
MCLENNAN

Neil was brought up in Seaton and Cotton Street, then moved to Kincorth when he was about fifteen. His father, Spunky McLennan was a well-known guy amongst the boxing booths, where he made a lot of money fighting.

Neil has been a single father for the last twenty plus years and brought up his three kids from ages one, three and five on his own while still being able to travel to different countries to work.

My father always told me if a guy ever pulls a weapon on you, run like fuck because you can always come back and get him another day, but if you stay you might not be able to.

At school, I was very quiet and timid and can't remember ever having a fight before moving to Kincorth. It all started when one day at school, I was playing table tennis in the hallway, these two brothers came up to me and started giving me a hard time, I just lost it and knocked fuck out of the pair of them. After that day, the guys in the school were all saying, "Fucking hell, that McLennan isn't the quiet guy we thought he was."

1982, I was working in Dundee as a scaffolder with a few other Aberdeen guys. I went to view this big house which had about six flats inside, the lassie said to me, "Oh, this one is fifty and this one is sixty." I stopped her in her track and said, "Fuck it, I will take the lot." We all moved in and stayed there for about two years, it was a rough part of Dundee and in that day, there were a few hard fuckers in there.

One night, a few of us were down at the pub having a few swallows, there were a few Glasgow guys with us, Tam Young and a few others. This Big Fucker approached me and said, "Hey, you! you're shagging my bird!" I asked who his bird was, because I didn't know, he shouts, "You know her Ok! She works in the Ronda-View, your Neil McLennan and you're shagging her!"
I said, "Oh yeah, I know her, I'm not shagging her, but I've been trying to, and I will shag her one day!"
He furiously said, "Ok me and you, lets sort this out in the toilets." So off we went and as I got into the toilet two of his mates appeared, one of them was a little skinhead guy with a scar down the side of his face, I always remember what my father said about guys with scars on their faces. *It's not them you got to worry about, it's the cunts that put it there!* Anyway, I'm now in the toilet with three of them, D.S a good friend of mine came over and said, "there's three of them, so I've come to back you up,"

I said to him, "I don't need you, but stand outside and watch the door."

I got torn into the fuckers and the blood was everywhere, it was like a war zone. I knocked the first one out cold, the next one, I knocked clean through the door and the third one I left lying in a pool of blood. I had Bit off the guy's ear and every time I went out, the bouncers used to put their hands over their ears, for a laugh.

D.S came running in and said, "What the fuck, you better get out of here!"

I washed the blood off my hands and face and as I walked back to my table the guys said, "Where the fuck have you been? Are you alright Neil? Who the fuck did that?"

I said, "It's ok boys, I'm fine" next thing, these two bouncers came over and asked who the fuck had done that in the toilets, the guy who I just done in, came over to the bouncers and said, "It's OK, it wasn't all this lot it was just him on his own, so just let him be." After that night they nicknamed me the 'Tasmanian devil' and every night we went out to the night clubs in Dundee we just got to walk straight in without paying a penny.

Working in another place called Broughty Ferry, there was a pub called the Ferry Inn, owned by a guy called Jeff Stewart. We went to book in and the guy apologised as he had double booked the room, he sent us down to Monifieth where his son ran the Panmure Hotel, it was very posh. There was a wedding on at the time and it was very busy, but he managed to give us one room with a few beds in it. At night we went to town and when we got back we were pissed, but still on the look for more drink, the owner left us to help ourselves and then headed off to his bed. We then noticed this big fish tank, so I went and got myself a carrot, sliced it up to look like fish and sneakily dropped them in the tank, I then shouted over to my mates, "hey! watch me eat this fish" I picked a carrot out and swallowed it, next thing these two Big Fuckers came running over and started growling at me, "What the fuck you doing?"

I told them I was only joking but they still weren't happy with me. Back down at the bar again and we were well wrecked with the drink, I went over to the tank again and done the same thing, except this time it was a real fish. My mates were egging me on to swallow it, I just did it for a laugh and to piss the two guys off, they came over to attack me, so I just threw the biggest fucker to the ground and decked the other one.

I was offshore with Richard Dunn, who was also a 'scaffolder', he was the ex-heavyweight boxer who fought Mohamed Ali. He used to carry four thirteen-foot scaffold boards at once, he was some size of a guy. Me and him went to the gym together and he got me to hold the punch bag for him, he about knocked me flying every time he punched the bag, so he taught me how to stand and hold the bag the proper way.

It was my turn to punch the bag, I was giving it my best shot and never forgot Richards words *'Aye loon you can fairly throw a punch'*, coming from a guy who fought Ali it made my day! He said, "Neil, you should try out boxing with that punch"

I said, "No, I'm into my football,"

His reply, "Oh, that's a 'poof's' game, get into boxing." Richard had his own sparring gloves and what a fucking size they were, as he had hands like shovels.

Richard taught me a lot about how to fight and said it doesn't matter how big or small someone is, if you hit them on the right spot you will rattle their brain and knock them off balance. He told me about the day he fought Ali and how he was all excited, Ali got interviewed about the fight and was boasting about what round he would knock Richard out. Richard said, "Round one...I was punching him and doing well, this went on for four rounds and I was thinking *fuck me I'm doing brilliant,* then Ali whispers in my ear... "Richard it's time to go" and the next thing I remember was getting knocked about" I worked with Richard for about a year until one day he fell and smashed himself up badly.

On holiday in Spain with little Jim Knowles, we were at this bar and I decided to go to the toilet, as I was standing having a piss in walked these two English fuckers, all dressed up in their England tops and Union Jack gear. Next thing this fucker was pissing over my shoes! I said, "Oi! Watch what the fuck you're doing!"
he replied, "Oh fuck off you Jock cunt."
Well... I head-butted him and then his mate jumps on me, so I battered the fuck out of him too, I didn't stop until there was blood everywhere. I walked out of the toilet with just a little bit of blood on me, went over to the bar and told my mate I had just wiped out this pair of English fuckers.
Next thing, the cops come in, the lights are all turned up and they get everyone up against the wall, then they started to let folk leave and as I was walking out the door I put my hand on Jimmy Knowles to say *thank fuck we got away with that* but noticed I must have had blood on my hands as it was all over Jimmy's shirt. The police noticed the blood on Jimmy's shirt and grabbed him, Jimmy shouts, "What you doing? It wasn't me, it was him!" they marched us out and into this little Fiat car . We were in the back seat with coppers all around us, with their guns in full view, *(quick thinking)* I started to hide all my money in my socks just in-case they stole it from me. Jimmy was now panicking and asking me where they were taking us, I said, "it's ok, most likely they will take us somewhere, beat us up and throw us out."

Now we are well outside the outskirts of Benidorm, I turned to Jimmy and said, "I'm getting a bit worried now," Jimmy started crying and said, "For fuck sake! I knew I shouldn't have come on holidays with you." We now stop out in this wood, I look over and spot this little wooden hut, I was thinking *fuck me they are going to do us in!* Machine gun in our backs, they marched us up to this hut, opened the door and there was this fucker sleeping with a coat over his head. They turn on the lights and this guy got up. He must have been high up in the police as he had badges pinned all over his uniform. He started to ask us what happened, and as we were explaining he called us 'English men.' Well, Jimmy shouts, "Hey you! We are not English we are Scottish!" I began to tell him what happened, I said I was in having a piss when in walked two English guys, they pissed on my shoes and then called me a Spanish cunt. The officer went off on one and said, "Don't you call me a Spanish cunt!"

I explained, "No-No the guys called me a Spanish cunt,"

he said, "Oh, you no English?"

I said, "No, I'm Scottish!" little Jim started getting bold and said, "yeah we are Scottish" and shows him his Scottish tattoos.

The cop said, "Yeh Scottish? You got Scottish whiskey?" luckily for us, I had a bottle of whiskey back in my apartment. I said, "Yeh, I have whiskey back in my apartment,"

he then turned around and said, "We take you home and tomorrow I come to see you and you show me your passport and give me your whiskey."

Next morning there was a bang on the door and it was two coppers with machine guns and the officer was behind them. I Took them in and handed him a bottle of grouse and showed him our passports. He then said, "Thank you my friend, no problem, you good man I no like English, the man in the hospital no good, jaw broken, and eye socket smashed, but we can't find who it was that done it"

Jimmy was showing off saying, "yeah it was us" LOL. We were there for a month and loads of times the coppers would stop us and say, "Hey our Scottish friends, do you want a lift anywhere?"

One night I was sitting in the Scotsman bar in Benidorm when a riot started, A bunch of English guys were outside and started kicking this Scottish cardboard cut-out up and down the street, Scottish guys started fighting with them inside and outside the pub. One guy got stabbed and after they left, the pub was in some mess, the owner started cleaning things up, so I gave him a hand.

The next morning, he said, "Neil, have you ever worked in a bar?"

I said, "No, but I know how to pour a pint" He then offered me a job working behind the bar and I ended up staying there for a year.

I was in the Bridge bar one night with this well-known guy who was very dangerous with a blade. A couple of guys started annoying him and he was about to start fighting with them, but I told him just to ignore them and leave it be, as he would listen to me. After another couple of drinks in walked these two big Celtic supporters who started to get on his nerves, they then started to aggravate me, I told them to fuck off and that we didn't want any hassle as we were just out having a few quiet beers. We finished our beers and went up to the Grill bar to get away from the pair, but after a while the two fuckers walked in and started giving us shit again. My mate was getting even more angry, I calmed him down and told him to forget it.

Off we went to another pub, (The Star and Garter) we didn't even get half way through our beer and in walked the two Celtic fuckers again. Once again we left and headed down to the Royal Hotel, they didn't turn up there, so we thought we had seen the last of them. Obviously, they were just out looking for trouble.

We went back to the Bridge Bar and fuck me in they came, I got one of them in the toilet and knocked the shit out of him, as I was holding him down the fucker stuck his fingers in my eyes and I just lost it! I made a right mess of him. They left the pub and I looked around to see where my mate was but there was no sign of him, I could hear police and ambulance sirens everywhere. My mate had gone after them and stabbed them both. He ended up doing a few years in the jail for that.

My first night working On the doors at the Yates pub with Govie, There was a carry on and I was told to go over and sort it out, I went over to this guy and said, "Ok pal, drink up, you need to leave" the guy said, "You think?" he then tried to hit me with a bottle but luckily he didn't connect so I marched him outside and told him not to come back.

My first Sunday on the door and up walked this two big Yanks, they were pissed so I told them they couldn't get in. The big guy hit me with a cracking right hand and I landed over a car bonnet, I got up and decked the pair of them. As I was knocking the fuck out of one, the police arrived. I got lifted and that was the end of my door career as I lost my license.

In the Palace one night and this guy punched this lassie, there was blood everywhere, So I went over to him and asked what the fuck he was doing, he basically told me to Fuck off! So, I went over to tell the bouncers and they did fuck all about it.

At the end of the night the guy headbutted another woman who happened to be my daughter's school teacher. I approached the guy and we were rolling about the street punch for punch and then, I remembered an old trick I learned from this guy in my local pub, I was being a pain in the arse and this guy called Billy Ironside stuck his two fingers in my eyes and they were sore for days, I thought *fuck, I will have to remember that one.* Anyway, I about took the guy's eyeball out, my thing was if I'm fighting, I'm fighting to win so anything goes. The guy got up and started running, so I ran after him and got to him outside the Palace door. I noticed he had ripped my new leather jacket, I made such a mess of the guy that I got nine months in prison for it.

I got five years in jail for the Kincorth riot, I was only twenty-one at the time and it was my first time in jail. I was taken down by bus to Edinburgh Stockton to get assessed to see what jail I was going to. We had to get a small test to see how bright or thick we were. This guy I knew turned to me and said, "Neil, you don't want to be going to Glasgow or Edinburgh jail, you would be better going up to Peterhead as its closer for visitors and that. What to do is refuse to do the test and they will send you on the green bus straight to Peterhead."

They handed me the test paper, I refused to do it and off to Peterhead I went. In a hall at Peterhead, I only lasted four days because it was something else, I must admit I was shitting myself because one day in the shower this guy was standing there watching me, he didn't say anything, but it was just the way he looked at me. I went up to see the governor and told him I had made a big mistake and asked if I could I get moved somewhere else. I ended up in Barlinnie and then on to Edinburgh.

My first night in Edinburgh jail and I was locked up on the bottom floor section where all the Beasts and Nutters were. It was a Thursday night and they opened the doors at the bottom section first, so we could go and watch the TV in the cinema room. A guy I knew shouted, "Neil keep me a seat because top of the pops is on at seven and you will get in there first" I got in and there were a couple of seats at the front, I put my feet on them to keep for my mate.

The place started to fill up and for some reason no-one sat down at the front with me, but after a while, two guys walked up and sat on either side of me. This big Glaswegian guy walked up and looked at the two guys and said, "What's going on and who the fuck is that?" he looked at me and said, "Hoy! you're on my fucking seat!" me, being a cheeky fucker, looked under the seat and said, "Sorry pal, I can't see your name on it",

"Oh, so you're a fucking 'wideo'? you cheeky wee cunt! Now get to fuck off my chair!" he said. At that point there were two screws in the cinema room, one at the front and the other standing next to the riot bell, the Glasgow cunt threw his cup of boiling hot tea in my face and punched me straight on the nose. I fell over and then got up and grabbed him while his two sidekicks were having sly digs at me. I wasn't getting the better of the big fucker, so I knocked him on his arse and picked up a metal table. I kept smashing it off his back until he crawled under some tables. I then chased after his two sidekicks and started making a mess of them, at that point all the cons were shouting at the screws, "If you push that emergency bell, you will have a riot on your hands!" so that was the end of the three Glaswegian fuckers.

69

I was sent to this cell which was in darkness and fucking filthy. The next morning the door opened, and I was told to wash up as the Governor wanted to see me. I got 'frog-marched' up there and ended up losing it with the screws, then I was thrown back into this fucking stinking cell, this went on for three days. The next day this guy walked in and said, "Hi I'm (such and such) from Aberdeen, I noticed you haven't got off to a good start here since you arrived from Peterhead, would you like to work in the engineer shop with me? All you have to do is go see the governor and agree with everything he says, and I will get you working with me as it's the best job to get in this jail."

I asked why he was doing that for me and he said, "because you're an Aberdeen guy like myself and I hate that Cunts as well, by the way, You are a hero with all the cons now after sorting out that three, no-one liked them and couldn't get near them."

When up in front of the governor, he said to me, "Oh my, the little lad has learned some manners" I felt like telling him to fuck off but held my tongue. Thirty day's recreation, thirty day's activities, no visits for thirty days and locked up in solitary for thirty days.

I was in my cell and this guy knocked on my door and said, "Hello, I'm big Geordie McKay can I come in?"

I said, "Aye, in you come."

He said, "I'm Geordie McKay, I'm doing a life sentence and I run this place, so we are not going to get any trouble from you are we?"

I said, "No, I just keep myself to myself,"

He said, "Good! And by the way, thanks for sorting out that fucker's the other day, we have been trying to get hold of them for months." He looked over and said, "You see all that clothes you got over there? Well get rid of them and come with me," he took me through to the clothes store and said, "Ok, what size of shirt are you?" I got new sets of clothes, new pillows and new sheets, the lot. "You're now one of the boys," he said and then took me downstairs to meet all his gang Ian

Taylor, Alex Wright, Harry Jasper, Drew Heenie, Bill and Jim Kenny, they nicked named me furry boots for some reason and I ended up loving the place.

Neil was a regular follower of the tartan army and travelled all over the world to see Scotland, he played the drum at the front of their marches, he couldn't actually play the drums though, he would just bang on them.

One day Scotland got beat and as we came out of the game at Amsterdam I threw my drum into a canal, with great joy to my friends as they were sick of me banging on them. Sitting at the globe bar Amsterdam and in walked this guy shouting, "Hey Rambo, we got your drum out of the lake"

My mates were all moaning, "For fuck sake, we thought we got rid of that Fucking thing!"

When I was in Slovenia I threw my drum on the pitch and Darren Fletcher picked it up and started banging on it. The sun newspaper picked up on this story and bought me another one. The Scotland Physio found the drum in the dressing room and got all the players to sign it, and now it's sitting in the Chelsea cabinet room as the Physio is now at Chelsea.

DOD MOORE

Dod was born and brought up in Torry, he missed out on most of his teen years as he spent a lot of his time in borstals and jail. He then went on to serve some years in the army until he left at the age of twenty-one. He spent all that years taking orders from officials in the army, he had to learn to stand up for himself as he would get a bad time being known as an *"Aberdeen Sheep Shagger"* Something Aberdonians were called by people from the South.

When I was in jail I was only about nine stone and after a few fights with the Glasgow wide men, I soon grew up. I had made up my mind that when I got released I wasn't going to let anyone fuck with me.

In the 50's down at the Carnivals they used to have a boxing booth and I remember when I was ten, Bobby Broke and I went into the ring to have a fight knowing that after the fight, the crowd would throw money in the ring for the younger boxers. Well... have you ever tried to pick up money with boxing gloves on? I managed it with one hand while peeling an orange in my pocket with the other LOL.

I Remember a day down in the Timmer market back in 1962 this guy called Frugal stuck the head on this guy who was about 6ft. It was quicker than fucking lightning, what a speed! Ginger McColl always said that the guy Frugal was the, 'one to watch' even though he was as heavy as a wet woodbine and only 5ft 4.

The Castle Hill barracks was where a lot of Hard-Men came from, another two names, Denis McDonald from Torry (R.I.P) and Ginger McColl both born in the barracks.

They should have sent the fucking Germans in there, as there was not a hope of escaping out of there, some of the women were even worse.

My sister Margaret, she could handle herself. When she was sixteen she would look after me and my brothers and there was nothing she was afraid of. One day down at Simmies shop on the 'Manser' there were these two guys hitting Robert and me, Margaret went down and punched them both, then wrapped their bikes around their fucking necks.

One night I met this bird at the Wednesday Grab a Granny night at the Palace, She stayed beside the Dancing Cairns pub, we stayed in bed all day as I was a bit of a 'Shagger' in my days *Hahaha*, anyway we nipped in by the Cairns that night and they had a darts match on, they were getting beat and I shouted, "Come on the Covies!" Well next thing, there were chairs and tables getting thrown about everywhere, some cunt just missed my head with one of that old fashioned thick glass ashtrays, if it had hit me I would have been out like a light. Next thing, police cars and vans everywhere, so a good night then and back to the birds' house to give her more joy LOL.

One time in the 70's or 80's when the Tanfield bar was the old Tanfield, I had a bit of trouble with a few of the local (gentlemen) there. I said to Ginger McColl, "I'm going up to the Tanfield to see what the score is" I had battered a certain local guy from there and they wanted my blood. They wouldn't come down to see me in Market Street, so I thought I would brass it and go to them. Ginger being my best pal said, "I'm coming with you" We got a taxi up there and when we got in we sat with our backs to the wall. There was a right dirty dodgy lot that came in with objects hidden in their coats, we got it sorted out and after that, they invited us back to a party in Logie, but we declined.

Times I tried for ages to walk away but no, the gunslingers wanted your boots so there was only one-way to go. Time and time again I got arrested and charged, god I was hard done by *Hahaha*.

Jim Broon, Denis, Bosco Adams and myself all worked in the Guild hotel as peacemakers, it was the only pub that opened when Celtic and Rangers came to visit. After the game they would all head for the Guild before they got on their train back to Glasgow. It was always mobbed and most of them were arseholes.

They had one guy there who was their leader. Denis worked behind the bar and asked me to help him because they were so busy. Well, my girlfriend Vicky at the time worked in the lounge, so the leader of this lot said, "I will keep this lot under control if I get a few free drinks." Well, it wasn't my stock, so the guy had free drinks all night. I never went to the till the whole night, I just charged them to the nearest pound and put the money straight in my hipper.

In the lounge, Vicky started the night with a 36DD bra and ended up with a 40DD lol. After that, we went to a bed and breakfast and emptied all the money that was in her bra, my pockets, and my socks. We made a fortune while Denis, Bosco and Jim were working their arses off, the boss even got them a carry out for their hard work *Ha*! The moral of the story is... there is an easy way to do bouncing and a hard way.

Charlie Small was also a doorman at the Guild. We had some battles in the Guild hotel.

Royal Atheneum, the pub on the corner across from the court it was a Saturday afternoon and I was having a drink with Jim Walker and Jim broon, (Not the boxing brown) this guy starts to slag off one of my

Craigie mates Ashley Craig, so I teold him to, "wrap up" and like a shot he says, "Ok Dod Moore, me and you outside!"

We went outside to the ABC car park and this guy was all over me like a rash. I had just spent the last five years on "holiday", I had only been home for a month. I was only twenty-one and the guy was in his thirties, the fight lasted about half an hour or so, I hit him with a bin lid.... nothing, so I hit him with the fucking bin and still no joy! His eyes were nearly closed, and he had a burst lip. He smoked a lot and was older than me, I think that's the reason I was able to beat him as he was one Hardy Fucker. I went back in the pub to finish my pint and then home to get cleaned up. His name was Danny, he was one of the hardest guys back in the sixties and that was my longest and hardest fight ever.

The minute you beat a well-known fighter everyone wants your badge and it's like the 'ok coral' every week and that's how things started.

Back in the days on Market Street and around the Lunar 7 when it was on the go, a few guys moved down from Glasgow and thought they would take over, but Ginger M^ccoll, Bopter, Larry Ford, Sandy Gibson and a few others said, "No way are they fucking going to take over!" They were told straight about that, but as years went on we all became good friends. Danny was a bit like me (R.I.P) he had a huge Tadger and would fuck anything with a pulse *Hahahahaha*!

I worked on the rigs with Rab and Jim Murray, I had a wee stramash with him but all palls after that. Also, Mick Carr a pure toff but what a poser and loved himself, also Joe Mackaleer he was a Glasgow version of myself we the birds LOL.

There was this guy that worked as a doorman at the lunar 7 and as a board marker at the bookies on Market street. One day me, Ginger McColl, Larry Ford, Bobby Flood, Johnny Dyker, Ritchie and another guy called Jackie (another hard-man I fought with) were in the bookies. Me and the doorman from the lunar 7 had an argument and he said that he was going to throw me out of the bookies, I said, "Wait till the racing finishes then we will go behind the bookies to the lane at the back." As we were walking out to go round for a square go Ginger said, "Dod this guy is no mug, he is a one hit man!" I thought *well if it happens like that it will be over quick,* as we went around the back I sensed the hand coming and moved to the side, well fuck me, the sound of the wind with his fist as it passed me. Well then, I was all over him and BUMP! BUMP! BUMP! He had a bad left eye, so I poked my finger in it and then he just slid down between two cars. That was the end of him.

There was this guy big Norman who was the bouncer at the Moorings and Eddy Caron who were both British Navy boxing champs and not a pair to fuck with. Ronnie Ritchie from Seaton, he was top-notcher at St Margaret's in the Castlegate.

On my first week out of the army after serving five years I went up to see my brother Jimmy and sister Margaret and as I walked onto the dance floor Ronnie put his arm out and told me I had to go under it, well no fucking way, so that was me and him rolling about the floor. After that day Ronnie and I became good mates and we would drink together down at the looking glass. His big brother Dod was a hardy guy too.

One time in the Argo which was the place to go in the days after the Moorings. the guy that owned it (Dougie Argo), which older dockers would know had a wooden leg and could still look after himself. Well this night me and my girlfriend Vicky was having a wee quiet drink on our own and as we looked over, these three guys were having an argument with Dougie because they were barred from the club.

That night Dougie had a doorman on but when he saw trouble brewing up he slipped into the toilet. Well, one of the guys hit Dougie and because of his leg, he fell to the floor. I couldn't just sit there and do nothing, so I ran over and decked the nearest one and then went for the second one, by this time Dougie got up and decked the third and that was the end of that three guys, so it was a free drink for Dod every time Dougie saw me.

Dougie also owned the Palace nightclub and told his bouncers to let me in for free anytime no matter how I was dressed or how drunk I was, I went in one night with my working clothes, balls hanging out and my face covered in cement, I remember meeting Gordon Grieve and me and him standing at the bar all night, my haversack and flask in the cloakroom and still managed to come out we a bird LOL, those were the days!

Some names from the eighties and nineties were Dennis and Bosco Adams fae Torry, Andy Ritchie from Northfield. When I was about sixteen we had Ginger McColl, Johnny Dyker, Ronnie Pirie and Ally Nelson, we were always up to something on Market Street.

Years ago, the Cheval Casino was the 'in' place to go after drinking hours it was mobbed every weekend. At that time Dick McGregor was the bouncer and he was a right Hard-Man.

Miller's bar you had Jim and Tam Brown, there weren't a lot of people who came out of Miller's bar without a black eye or bust head.
One of the kindest person I came across was Walter senior who was one in a million and who could also handle himself. When Walter was trawling when the fishing industry was booming, it was my sons Stevens' 5th birthday and I didn't have a lot of money at that time, so Walter took me to a big warehouse off of George Street and bought Steven a toy police pedal car, when I brought it home the little fucker just played with the box.

I had years of battles with a lot of people mentioned in the group and everyone knows the battles, but that was just the way it was back in the day.

I am 72 now and every other week my family phone me to tell me this and that person has died, some have lasted longer than most but there is a lot of good guys that died young. Yan Esson, Danny Sproul, Dennis Adams R.I.P, the list goes on. So I say you have to live your life to the full as much as possible, love and look after your closest friends and family as if it's your last day because you never know it might be.

JIM ROBERTSON

Jim grew up in Mastrick with his brothers Billy, Michael, Kenny, and his sister Hazel. Like most of us in those days they didn't have much money, his father was a trawlerman and his mother worked in the fish. In his early days at school he was never one to fight, he went to school with this 'Big Tackety Boots' on and everyone could hear him coming before they could see him, because of this he was nicknamed Tackety.

It wasn't until Jim got sent to borstal that he started toughening up and got into a few scraps. Jim was a great swimmer and footballer, he was picked to swim for Scotland but didn't turn up, and played first division amateurs as a youngster but quit his sports when he grew up and started going out drinking etc. He did return to football in his late twenties, scoring goals for fun and even won the Green final player of the year. Jim is sixty years old now and still keeps himself fit and over the years has went toe to toe with some of Aberdeen's hardest men.

When I started playing football again after Borstal, I played for Summerhill and we went on to win the Scottish Welfare Cup and bagged goals along the way. One of the games, I jumped up to head the ball and the next thing blood was pouring out of my head, the Physio ran over to clean me up and couldn't believe what he had found stuck in my head...Two teeth! I had stuck the head in a guy the previous night, I guess the teeth must have belonged to him.

Playing a friendly football match with Kincorth which was being watched by hundreds of people, because everyone thought it might all kick off, this well-known guy from Kincorth was screaming at all of us all through the game.

The game ended and as we were walking back to the dressing room this guy was sitting on the wall outside and smacked my mate on the side of his face, 'braking his jaw.' I said, "Fuck sake man that was out of order!"

He turned around to me and said, "Do you want the fucking same?" Well, I went straight for him and knocked him out in seconds, now I'm as high as a kite and went straight to their dressing room and booted the door in. They all ran off leaving socks, shorts, etc in their path.

> *"Summerhill v Torry Vics 1995ish, Jim went up to head the ball that I was away to hoof up-field, by accident I kicked him on the forehead I said, "Jim you ok?" he just looked at me and said "aye", then instantly an egg appeared on his forehead and I said, "fuck sake, you need to get that seen to!" his response, "I'm fine" as he carried on playing, most people would have been knocked out and carted off to hospital. Tough as teak."*
> **-Mike McBain**

Jim spent most of his youth at young offenders and borstal, when he got released at seventeen from Glenochil's his first job was a bouncer on the doors.

One day when Biff and I were bouncers at the Lodge, three guys came walking in. One of the them was a Big Fucking Body Builder. After a few drinks they started to get out of hand throwing bottles on the floor. Biff went to ask them to pick the bottles up and they told him to fuck off! I went over to ask them, and their reply was the same, Fuck

80

off! That was enough! Biff and I got torn into them, I knocked one of them out, dragged him by the hair, threw him in the lift, pressed the button and shouted, "Ground Floor!". Years later when I would walk into the Lodge folk would shout "Ground Floor!".

"One Sunday night I ventured up to the Summerhill lodge where Jim Robertson was the doorman, as I walked in the bar I could hear them all growling saying, "What the fuck is DOD Moore doing in here?" they wanted me out. Jim as always, took me to the bar and we had a few drinks, later we went upstairs to the disco and had a great night. Jim and I got on well ever since then, Jim said he bought all the drinks but he was accused of buying a round but found not guilty as there were no witnesses and no previous convictions for that lol, also I told him he had to go to spec-savers as he said he was better looking than me lol at that time I had more birds than an aviary." - **Dod Moore**

At nineteen years old I was down at the Inverdon pub and got into a

81

brawl with this guy. I ended up getting the better of him and admittedly, I knew I went over the top by knocking the guy out. The Police and Ambulance arrived and put a white sheet over the guy and I honestly thought the guy was dead!

I ended up in court with attempted murder, but thankfully the guy made a full recovery and I only got an eighteen-month sentence. I now get on great with the guy.

I was about 26 years old and sitting in the pub. The night before, two well known guys and friends at the time, had a big fight. One of the guys walked into the pub with a black eye and said to me, "I will give you a grand if you batter the shit out of the guy that did this to me" I'm thinking, *the guy he wants me to do this to, is a guy I know well and like a lot.* I said, "OK" so off to the bank he went. He came back and handed me the money.

This was in the eighties and I had never saw a grand in my life, anyway, I got home with the money and my phone rang it was the other guy who I had just been paid to do in. "I heard you were offered a grand to do me in, look son I can't be arsed with this nowadays, if you come down and see me, I will give you a grand not to start anything." I thought it was a set up, so the guy sent a taxi to take me down to the pub he was drinking in. I walked in and he handed me a grand, I'm now thinking *how I get out of this one,* sitting with two grand in my pocket thinking I'm the richest fucker in Aberdeen. Well next thing the other guy walked in to the pub and my heart missed a beat thinking *Oh Fuck!* But the guy heads over to the guy he was fighting with the night before and they both start hugging each other and saying how sorry they were about the night before.

I'm thinking *fuck this, they are not getting their money back,* the guy winks over to me as if to say its OK forget about the money and the other guy came over and whispered to me, "It's OK now, just forget

82

what we planned but still keep the money." I was two grand richer and never even had to lift a finger. *Hahahaha*!

Growing up as a kid, my hero was Bopter McCrae, I learned so much from him. Most people who knows Bopter, would say the same about him...He was just a machine!

Troopers bar, me and Bopter were having a quiet pint and a game of pool. Across from us was another well-known guy from Torry sitting at a table with a few of his mates. After a while up at the bar the guy walked over to me and said, "You're my milkman, are you?" probably because I was wearing a white shirt, I said, "Sorry mate you have got the wrong guy." Unknown to me Bopter's watching all this and says to a few guys just watch this as he knew the guy was being wide with me. I didn't, I just thought the guy made a mistake, the guy then repeated himself, "Are you sure you're not my milkman?"

"I'm not your fucking milkman!" I shouted. I smacked him, before he hit the deck I booted him right on his mug and knocked him clean out,

Whitehorse pub one-afternoon Bopter, Ronnie Boyle, Johnny Lawrence, English guy called Paul Dabell and myself walked in and I said to Paul, "If you're playing pool don't take off your jacket or it will get nicked," After a while I was playing three card brag with a few of the locals who I knew from jail when Paul came over and said, "Jim they have nicked my jacket!"

I said, "For fuck sake what did I tell you? what do you want me to do, search everyone? Next thing this guy walked over and tipped the pool table up and all hell broke loose. I grabbed the kitty put it in my pocket and said, "OK let's get into them!"

I was fighting a few of them, I looked over and there was Ronnie smashing up the gantry with a chair. I looked over the other side and there was Bopter standing watching me. I shouted, "Hey! any chance of a hand here?" there were more and more of them, and I was under seige as two of my mates were down and Ronnie was still smashing up the bar. Bopter shouted back at me with a smile on his face and said, "No, No, you're doing OK." Next thing, he walked over and I swear on it, he battered five of them within minutes, I looked over to Ronnie again and said, "Fuck sake man, at least grab the till!" then we left with bodies lying everywhere.

*It was a Sunday and my mate and I went up to our local (The Summerhill Lodge) we were standing at one end of the bar and Jim and his mate were standing at the other end, in walked two English guys, one of them was being a pain in the arse and started rambling on a load of shit to us, he decided to go further down the bar and nip Jim's head...Next thing, Jim sticks the nut on him and sends him flying into the pool table and as he hit the ground he got a volley in the head for good measure. The young guy said to Jim, "You better get to fuck out of here, as the boys got a serious head injury!" the English guy was bald and his head was all black and bruised, the barmaid came out with a damp cloth to try and revive him, she placed it on his head and the blackness started running, it ended up it was the boot polish off Jim's boots that was on the boys head. - **Unknown***

Many times, Jim would be sitting at home watching TV with his feet up when the phone would ring, and it was one of his friends or family who was having a bit of bother down at the pub.

One day a good friend of mine phoned and said, "Jim, there's these three guys who came into the pub yesterday, and they've came back in today and they keep staring at me, I'm getting a bit worried." I got dressed and ran down to the pub only to find out that the three guys came from Raeden Special Needs School, they had gone up to the pub

the previous day and witnessed my mate 'Bleezing' drunk and he had been singing and dancing about everywhere. They thought this was great. They only went back that day to see the entertainment again, but unfortunate for them he was standing quietly sober while they kept looking over at him waiting for his performance
.

One day I came out the pub with the Mrs, who was pregnant at the time and we were on our way to get a Chinese carry out. I looked over and there were two guys who were just waiting to pounce on me. I told the wife to stay behind a tree and promised her she would get her Chinese. I went over and knocked the two guys out cold, I kept my promise to the wife though, I got a Chinese for her.

I Was in jail once when this Aberdeen guy was picking on these Glasgow guys and stole their dinner, I said, "Fuck sake, give the guys back their dinner!" well, we got into a heated argument and I said, "OK me and you back in my cell" at that point there was a big audience and they started taking bets on the fight. I was only a small guy and this guy was huge! so all the Glaswegian's were putting all their bets on the big guy, thinking I had no chance. Sitting back watching all this was Johnny Leslie who was in borstal with me and knew me very well, so Johnny pipes up, "OK you lot, I will take all your bets as I'm backing the small guy." *Hahaha*! All I will say is Johnny made a fortune that day.

Grampian bar, me and Mike McGuire standing at the bar having a few drinks and in walked this big well-known guy from Torry, he started shouting out, "I will fight any cunt in this bar!" he then walks over to the bar and picks on Mike, so Mike picked up this water jug and smacked it over his head, but the guy just shrugged it off. Next thing, the guy was having a go at me, so I went outside with him and knocked him clean over and made a right mess of him. He landed in the middle of Victoria road with buses and cars swerving to avoid him. The police and ambulance pulled up and I took to my heels and had a lucky escape.

*One day I will never forget, it was a Saturday afternoon in my local and the pool room was mobbed, Jim was sitting in the far away corner with some of Aberdeen proper hard-nuts Ricky Turner, Bopter, etc., well in came this guy. I knew he was looking for trouble, and like every other local pub he was being watched very carefully by some. Anyway, this guy goes around every table just being an arse, I said to my lot, "fuck me, when he gets to Jim Robertsons' table they are going to kill him!" Well, for some reason he got past them without a word being said. He then got to our table and started his shit! I jumped over the table, kicked the shit out of him and then got thrown out of the pub. The next time I spoke to Jim he told me that when the guy walked over to our table, he told his lot to watch as he knew I was going to go for him. What I have noticed over the years is when you go into someone's local and start speaking to the top guys in the pub even in deep conversation or having a laugh they are always watching what's going on around them." - **Mike Sheran**

BARRY LAING

Barry was brought up in Kincorth, he got his first pair of boxing gloves at the age of eight. The older guys used to make him box in the playing fields and bet money on the fights, he got a lot of beatings because they made him box against older boys.

Barry boxed for twenty-one years and fought semi-professional as a kick-boxer. He didn't get on very well with his parents because they thought he was a 'problem child' and they didn't know how to handle him.

At sixteen years old he had a massive fight with his father over something stupid, his fathers words were 'your now sixteen and I have been waiting for years to give you a good beating,' after that Barry moved into a drug dealers house on Logie Avenue and then got himself mixed up with the drug scene, running back and forth to Glasgow and Edinburgh, getting involved with some dodgy people. After a few years doing that, Barry started hanging about with the bikers, beating up the older boys in his area and started getting a name for himself.

It got to the stage that everyone was petrified of him, even his mates and his mother and father, at one stage he didn't even get invited to his 'mates' wedding because of what he became.

Barry couldn't understand why he was like that, then they got to the bottom of it and found out he had A.D.H.D. Barry always wondered why every time he would go into a pub, folk would buy him drinks, (*was it because they liked him or was they just scared of him?*) Barry asked his friend to answer him the truth, "why do you buy me drink is it because you're my friend or your scared of me?"
His friend's reply was, "oh I do like you but we are all very wary of you."

Barry got involved with the underground bare-knuckle boxing and travelled all over Scotland to fight. He was in this bar one day and got talking to this guy, he told him about the bare knuckles boxing, the guys mate challenged him outside for money. He went out to the car park and the guy put Barry on his arse, which was a shock to Barry's system. Barry got up and ended up knocking the fuck out of the guy, next thing, the guy that was holding the money hit Barry on the back of the head with a brick.

His next fight was down at Leith and was one of Barry's hardest fights ever, but he still made a mess of the guy, until yet again his mate hit Barry over the head with something while their other mates held a knife to Barry's friend's throat. They all jumped on Barry and kicked fuck out of him until he was unconscious. They broke his nose and cheekbone, he was taken to the hospital and then the police arrived to interview him and asked him to press charges against the other guy who was well known to them and they hated him. He also ended up in hospital, but Barry didn't press charges.

Back home again in Aberdeen he got arrested for stabbing a copper in the leg, they took him to 'Lodge Walk' and threw him in the cells, at that point he grabbed a copper by the throat and wouldn't let go of him. They ended up breaking his wrist so he would let go of the copper. He was in his cell and started to take out the stitching in his mattress, then pulled most of the foam out of it.

when his hatch was opened Barry jammed it with the foam and when the turn-key started pulling it from his end it jammed even more, and now leaving the mattress covering the back of the cell door, which left Barry time to hide behind so they couldn't see him.

By law when a hatch door is open they have to have someone there and not allowed to leave it unmanned, this went on for about 4 hours. All that time Barry didn't mutter a word, they had to call in the riot squad, about eight of them arrived with all the gear on, they gently opened his door, but didn't realise Barry was underneath it so he managed to escape into the corridor. When they caught up with him they all laid fuck into him until he was unconscious and he was left in a bad way.

He was charged with twenty-three police assaults and was classed as a dangerous custodian. Two days later the guy in charge of the riot squad walked into his cell to tell him that they would be holding his court appearance from his cell as he was too dangerous to take up into court. Barry thinks it was because they couldn't take him to court because of the mess they had left him in. The officer told him he had another option, if they took him up to the hospital to get fixed up and then let three police officers take him back to court without any trouble, they would drop a lot of his charges against him. Barry ended up getting nineteen months jail sentence

Three weeks after serving his jail sentence Barry was driving along the road when some guy just about crashed into his car, Barry gave the guy the middle finger and just carried on his way. He got to the bank at Greenwell Road and when inside, in came the guy that was in the other car and started with him. Barry ended up knocking the shit out of him inside the bank, which led to Barry serving another six months in jail.

After that Barry decided to get away from everything as he was worried that at some point he would end up killing someone. So off he went to America and travelled to many other countries, he didn't have much money when he left Aberdeen so he ended up sleeping rough on the streets of New York for about nine months. He then moved to a little town called Deerfield but had to leave there because he got involved in a massive brawl with some of the local guys. He then bought himself an old 5.7 Crown Victoria car for six-hundred dollars and drove all the way to Mexico. When he got there he got involved in a scuffle with the police and was thrown in jail for a few days. He then moved back to America, on to Jamaica for a few months, moved again to Peru for four months and then came back to Aberdeen .

My interview with Barry lasted over three hours with so many more very interesting and amazing stories which hopefully will be revealed in his own book at a later date.

Barry has changed his ways over the last few years and is disgusted with himself at the damage he has done to certain people and ruined their lives. He doesn't smoke and hardly drinks, he became a passive person and tries to back away from trouble in case he hurts someone badly. He spends a lot of time with his bikes and keeps himself 'fit as fuck.' He would stand toe to toe with anyone because he is a trained fighter, boxer and kick-boxer and is such a nice, genuine guy.

"One of the nicest guys to grace planet earth, Barry is a scholar and a gentleman."
                                        *- **Martin Buchan***

LEE HUTCHEON

I grew up in Woodside back in the 80s. Back then it was like something out of a fuckin Wild West film. Millers bar even had the cowboy swing doors with sawdust on the floor. Im sure there were fuckers walking in there with cowboy boots and spurs as well. Probably pawned them to Jackie Miller for bevvy later that night. Place was like a fuckin war zone back then! As kids we never had much but what we did have we always shared and everyone had each other's backs, you looked out for your pals no matter what and we would fight to the last man to protect one another. I've always been proud of where I come from. If it wasn't for my background and my upbringing then I would have never been able to go on and make films such as "In A Mans World' which I went on to do many years after. Most of the kids in our area ended up out on the street purely to escape the nut houses they were being brought up in. Half the mothers in Woodside were the scariest motherfuckers you ever seen in your life (No teeth, tattoos on their knuckles, hairs on their chest, the slippers on with the house coat and tickler hanging out the lips) you get the picture! Well no wonder the kids opted to freeze their nuts off out on the street, and pretty soon it wasn't long before a gang was naturally formed and with that obviously came the mischief that goes with the territory. We used to fight against all other areas and it didn't take long before you would see who's who. Aberdeen wasn't like other parts of Britain with the guns and the knives, no no we were quite content to beat the ever loving shite out of each other with our fists to pass the time. If ever any of our pals were beaten by their mothers boyfriends then we would simply unite together and deal with the fucker right there in the middle of the street for all to see. There was an old fashioned bobby on the beat called 'Sandy' that all the kids respected. He was like a social worker more than anything and was there to keep the kids out of trouble. Not only that but if you did cross him then he would simply put his size 12 boot right up your arse and that would be the end of it. A very effective form of policing that should still be applied today I might add. Anyhow, the gang fighting with other areas got that bad that they eventually took sympathy on us and donated the first all weather football pitch to Woodside. 'An all weather football pitch my arse' lumpy tarmac and fuckin dog shit sprinkled with broken glass. Half the kids were sliding about with fuckin tasseled mod shoes on. You'd try and take a shot and end up with a fuckin glue bag wrapped round yer ankle and the slip on hanging off the fence. So the pitch idea didn't work and it wasn't long before every fucker was back fighting again, boredom being the main driving force. As the years passed the fighting escalated throughout the areas as did the rivalry with other mobs and pretty soon some reputations began to form. It's just the way it was back then. You ran with your boys, you fought with your boys and you protected your boys no matter what. Then once that reputation starts there's no turning back. You protect you and yours at all costs. As that reputation grows you obviously then get these wanna be 'Attila the hun cunts' trying to test your resolve which then has to be dealt with straight away. Then you get the next 'Conan the Barbarian' motherfucker trying to test your capabilities and yet again you have to sort him out and then the next one comes along and then the next and from there on in it never fuckin stops! As the decades passed the situations only got bigger as did the arseholes and you simply had to deal with it!

Things were very different back then though as there's a lot more options for youngsters these days which is why I made sure my own kids got good careers and didn't make the same mistakes. I also think things like Boxing clubs are great for the kids getting off the street as well which pretty much saved me as a kid along with the cinema house where I could escape from the dog shit that surrounded us on the street. If anything Boxing is great for teaching the kids discipline, dedication and of course respect which is severely lacking among today's youth.

Over the past 25 years I've sorted out many 'situations' most of which I cannot discuss due to obvious reasons. There are some stories however that I can share with you which can only be described as scenes out of an 'Only Fools and Horses' sketch. . . .

F-F-F-Fuckin Russians

I was standing in a bar one day chatting to a bar maid I knew and I could see that there was this Monster of a man at the other side of the bar beating his chest and growling down at everyone that looked his way. The fucker looked like that Jaws out of one of those 'James Bond' films. Anyhow I'm chatting away n'all of a sudden the entire fuckin room goes completely dark. I thought some fucker had turned out the lights but as I turned to my right I instantly realised that it wasnt the lights it was actually this huge fuckers shadow standing over me. So I'm thinking to myself, oh for fuck sake here we go, just keep drinking your pint Hutch, drink your pint, hes not there hes not fuckin there. Then all of a sudden I could feel him breathing down onto my neck. The entire boozer falls to complete silence, all I can hear is the bar maids glass sqeeking as she dries it. So I slowly turns towards this fuckin orangutan of a man as he lifts up his hand and pokes me hard in the chest. He sais...YOU! N' I went me? He went YOU! N'I went who me? He said YES YOU! YOU F-f-f-f-f-f-f-f -f-f. . . N'I'm standing there motionless as he tries again to say . . . F-f-f-f-f. . . So by this time the entire bar is standing motionless and I'm staring up at this fuckin cave man with his face all twisted and distorted going redder by the minute as he struggles to get this fuckin word out. I'm trying to act like everything is completely normal as his lip starts to quiver and sliver and still he cannot get this fuckin word out. Blubbering, gibbering, slobbering, sweating and they always say its never right to finish the word of a person who has a stutter but now this is becoming un-fuckin-bareable to watch because the clock is now ticking, the glasses are squeeking, the punters are frozen fuckin stiff and 'Jaws' is almost passing out because he cannot get this fuckin word out. It was unbareable, I couldn't take it anymore so I kindly said to the man, you mean f-f-f-f-fight? and he said Y-Y-Y-YES and I went BUMP right on his chin!!!! So now this fucker's standing staring down at me swaying back and forth, and I'm thinking, AH FUCK, HERE WE GO! . . . So the entire bar is still standing motionless as high tower's eyes begin to roll to the back of his head as he smiles down at me and then slowly but fuckin surely the tree trunk topples back and crashes to the floor with a thud, . . . and that was fuckin that!. . . . F-F-F-F-F-Fuckin Russians!!!

Scotland vs England

An old pal of mines from Aberdeen had moved down to London a good few years back and I was also down there at the time so we arranged to meet up. He drank in a famous East End boozer owned by the X-World Boxing Champion Charlie Magri who 'as it happens' was actually working behind the bar that night. This was a well respected boozer right in the heart of Londons East End and it was visited by many well known London gangsters both past and present. Anyhow, I went down to meet him there and as I walked in he was standing there at the bar surrounded by 8 other lads all dressed up in their ponsey suits and ties. Now to let you understand, the last time I seen my mate he was standing with a boiler suit n hard hat on in the middle of an Aberdeen warehouse covered in shit n now he's standing holding court in an East End London mob bar with a knot in his tie the size of his fuckin head, swirling a glass of brandy, smoking a cigar n I'm like 'what the fuck's going on here like'. So I tries to pretend that everything is completely normal and I went and ordered myself a pint. 'Alright utchy my old boy, ow's it fuckin gown son' he sais. N I'm like 'Eh? Aye flike min'. Now I'm thinking to myself, hold on this cunts fae fuckin George Street min what's with the Bob Hoskins voice? So as I looks around me I starts clocking all this other muppets he's standing with sporting their fake tans n pin striped waist coats n I'm thinking to myself 'Have I just walked into a scene out of a Bugsy fuckin Malone film' because it was honestly like a piss take of that movie. So we said our hellos etc and I orders a pint and turns to one particular clown that he was standing with who was wearing a bright yellow fuckin tie that would scare you and I decides to at least make an attempt to break the ice and be polite. So I said to this boy I said 'So what is it you do yourself pal' n the fucker raises his eye brows n turns away from me. N' I'm like mother fucker! So I taps him on the shoulder n I asks him again. 'So what aboot yourself pal, what is it you're into?' N'he starts chewing his chewing gum with his hands deep in his pockets n he sais...'Well that's for me to know n you to find out mate'. N I said 'Come again?' . . . N he goes 'Hold up son you old bill or somink'. N' now I've slammed my pint down n' I'm thinking 'Cheeky wee bastard this eh'. So I slowly looks around me at everyone else in the bar and they're all whispering and hugging and patting each other on the back n shaking hands. N I looks up at my mate who's standing there laughing like some kinda constipated hyena emersed in his cigar smoke with his jewellery dangling all over the shop n I'm thinking 'have I fuckin missed something here or what'. So I just said 'fuck it'. N' I swaggers across to the dart board n picks up a piece of chalk. I then marches to the other end of the bar n starts to draw a long white chalk line right across the middle of the bar floor. Now I could see Charlie Magris wee head leaning over the bar thinking to himself 'what the fuck?' So slowly each of these clowns starts to turn towards me n I can hear them saying to my pal 'Oi oi, look, what the fuck's the jock cunt doing, he's off his fuckin trolley mate'. So in big bold fuck off capital letters I writes the words SCOTLAND on one side of the line and then ENGLAND on the other side of the line. Now by this time every fucker in the pub is standing way back from me because they do not have a clue what the fuck i'm about to do next. Eventually you can see all the other faces in the bar looking down at the floor in disbelief as I steps into the Scotland half. The 'Bugsy Malone' gang are now completely n utterly shitting themselves and of course my mates face is an absolute fuckin picture as I say to him . . . 'I know what side I'm on pal . . . What I need to know is . . . what side are you on?' . . . You could hear a pin drop as the expressions on every one of their faces changes. . . He's like 'Utch utch what the fuck you doing mate' . . . N'I said . . . 'Dont you fuckin Utch me you cunt. . . I'm Invading fuckin England what does it look like'. . . Well that was it I thought he was going to shit himself there n'then as I stood there asking his pals if they wanted to come n' invade Scotland. Anyhow, the moral of this story is . . . Stay the fuck away from England! . . . It's over rated.

A Good Nights Kip

A good few years back a close family member of mine had taken a right brutal

95

beating for no reason from this big fat horrible animal of a man who was a right nasty piece of work. This had happened on the Saturday night and I had only seen the extent of the damages to his face on the Sunday night by which time I had already had a good few sherries. Anyhow, the beating was that bad that he later had to have surgery to his face. So as soon as he had told me exactly what had happened I instantly decided to pay this fucker a visit. As I say I had already had a good few drams in me so looking back at it now this maybe wasnt the cleverest of ideas, however at the time it seemed like a wonderful idea so off I went. As I approached his house I could see his light was on so I slowly made my way up to the door. As I approached I could see that the front door was left half open. So I kindly invited myself in and made my way slowly up the stairs. As I opened the sitting room door I could see there was nobody there. So slowly I turns my head toward the bedroom door where I could hear the big fat smelly ugly oger faced motherfucker snoring n grunting in his sleep. So I slowly opens his bedroom door n there I am staring down at this piece of shit lying there in cuckoo land. Now, I wanted this scumbag to look me in the eye, I wanted the fucker to see me coming for him so to do anything to this baboon whilst he was still asleep was not really my thing. So I then starts trying to waken the prick up. He had a wee fish bowl beside his bed so I picks that up n slowly starts to pour it over his fisog, the fish are now flapping aboot his mooth n' still this fucker continues to gargle blubber a load aw shite in his sleep. So I then starts to hold his nose but no no no the mooth starts slurping n slivering. I'm then thinking to myself what the fuck kind of situation is this, this is a piss take, so I sits doon at the bottom of his bed to get my thoughts together n' remember I was pissed as a hatter at this point. So as I'm thinking away to myself n' I remember looking doon at this mattress I was sitting on saying to myself this is one comfy bed this fucker eh, no way this is unreal. N then I remember lying back onto the bed n saying to myself 'this bed is the fuckin business'. N' the next thing I realises I slowly opens my eyes n' it was the next fuckin morning!!!. N I'm like get the fuck oot aw here I've just gone n'fallen asleep on the boys memory foam thing. N as I turns to my right I sees the boys wife standing there screaming at me with an iron in her hand. Then I turns towards the boy as he opens his eyes n we're both cosied in the gether 'spooning'. So he absolutely shites himsel n jumps up n I'm now chasing him aboot the room giving him his tatties whilst his wifes trying to brain me with her iron n the whole thing was like something oot a fuckin 'Carry on' film . . . but the most important thing is the message was delivered successfully . . . and of course . . . ' I got a good nights kip!!!

Paddy Fuckin Swayze!

In the 90's Aberdeen must have been one of the only places in Britain where the doormen weren't all fully licenced which meant you always got at least one prick prancing around a doorway playing 'Patrick Fuckin Swayze' after watching 'Road House' 55 times the week before. Anyhow these arseholes used to be out just looking for fights and were pretty much a law to there own, and of course they would always pick on the weak and vulnerable. On this particular Saturday night I had stayed in to watch the kids but there was a few of my pals out in town. One of them (who I will not name) took a right beating from a huge bouncer in the toilets of a nightclub for no reason. Now this is a man that wouldn't hurt a fly and is the kindest softest person you'll meet and these bastards did a right number on him and he ended up in hospital. I got wind of this early Sunday morning and through another good doorman pal of mine was quickly able to get a name and address for the animal that did it. Much to my surprise I was given the address of a town house in Forest Avenue up in the West End, so I instantly knew there and then that this was most definitely one of those wanna be 'Patrick Swayze pricks'. So 9am Sunday morning I heads up to Forest Avenue and knocks on the door of this mansion and a woman (who looked and sounded the double of the queen I might add) answers the door in her cooking apron and sais in a very posh English accent . . . 'Oh hello there sir, how can I help you'. I said good morning, I'm looking for John. She then said, 'Why certainly, he's upstairs washing behind the old ears you know. Sorry and your name is?' Now I knew his pals name was Alan so I just said 'aye it's Alan here'. So then she shouts 'Oh Johnathan, oh johnathan dear, that's Alan at the door for you sweetheart'. I then hears him shout . . . 'Tell him to come in.' So the woman sais 'Alan why don't you come in and make yourself comfortable dear'. So I walks into the kitchen and there's

97

the father sitting at the table reading the fuckin 'Wall Street' journal. She then taps him on the shoulder and sais, 'Darling, darling this is Alan, Johnathan's friend. (The father looked like fuckin Donald Trump on Crack Cocaine). 'Pleased to meet you Alan' he said. Sit down come and join us'. So I sits down and the mother sais 'Are you hungry, are you hungry Alan. How about a lovely cooked breakfast to get you going for the day eh eh eh'. . . Now I could not fuckin help myself because the smell of this cooking was fuckin unbareable so I thought, aye fuck it, I'm in! . . . 'Yes that would be lovely thank you'. So there's me, sitting there waiting for 'Paddy Fuckin Swayze' to come downstairs and I'm getting ripped into this full English breakfast. Then the father pipes up 'So what is it you're into yourself Alan, stocks and shares?' And I'm thinking, stocks n 'fuckin shares?... So he's blabbin on about stocks n fuckin shares, n the mother's sitting there next to me whistling away knitting n I'm sitting there in the middle of this with tomato sauce all over my face. Then I hears the footsteps coming down the stairs and the kitchen door slowly opens to reveal the bald hero himself. Paddy-Fuckin-Swayze in the flesh baby! So he instantly glances across towards me sitting at the table and goes into the cupboard to get a plate. He then slowly leans his head back as the penny finally drops to find me sitting smiling up at him. The plate then smashes to the ground. His face has now instantly turned 99 shades of white as his mouth slowly opens and his bath towel drops to the ground to reveal this wee half inch pecker. I'm now mopping up the sauce with my bread and he's standing there shitting himself. 'Are you ok darling, good god you're shaking look at you, Johnathan what's wrong darling. Alan-alan, help him'. N' I said 'Oh aye I'll fucking help him alright. . . . I steps over towards him. He's standing there wi the tinky winky hangin oot, shaking like a leaf. 'The next time you lay a fuckin finger on my pal. . . then there will be no more fuckin warnings. I will simply cut that excuse of a tadger of yours aff n staple it to your fuckin forehead einstein. . . You hear me? . . . (Looking down at his half inch willie of his, I whispers) Besides . . . I don't really think you've got the stones for it son! . . . Do you?

Funnily enough, I never heard back from old Paddy after that.

I'm glad to say life is very different for myself these days running a business and raising a family but these stories always make me chuckle none the less.

All the best!

Hutch

WILLIAM
(BOPTER)
MACRAE

Every person that I have spoken to about this book all had the same thing to say '*I hope Bopters in the book*!' As he was some guy in his day, Jim Robertson states that he learned so much off this guy, and when people talk about him their words were 'fuck he was just a machine this guy.'

For years the Aberdeen boys were getting raped in jail from a certain guy or guys and their minders, who were doing life sentences. It was unbelievable and getting out of hand. Until one day this twenty-three-year-old Northfield guy who got sent down for three years finally put a stop to it. They made a bad mistake and started on Bopter. He ended up kicking the guy and his minders all over the place.

Bopter got transferred to Peterhead prison which was full of Glasgow guys headed by the top guy at the time who was Glasgow's Jimmy Boyle. When Bopter arrived, the Glaswegians walked past him and said, "hoy! big man, the knives are getting sharpened for you!" and if you went near Jimmy Boyle at that time you would have been stabbed.

Bopter was some football player in his time, so one day Boyle walked up to Bopter and said, "hey big man they tell me you're a great football player, would you like a game for our football team?"

Bopter had a game for Boyle's football team and after the game he told Bopter, *'he was some football player and the knives were getting sharpened for him, but not now!'*

Bopter got a mention in Jimmy Boyle's book about the boy from Aberdeen that he wouldn't want to mess with.

"Bopter looked after me when I worked in the Cairns pub as he was a friend of my dad's. I witnessed him one day knocking a guy clean out with one headbutt. Bopter used to like coming in the Cairns to read his newspaper and this day this guy started taking the piss out of him and trying to act so hard in front of him, so Bopter started laughing and joking with the guy at the bar, the next thing the guys lying on the floor out cold."- Nicky Wright

"Bopter was not to be taken lightly"
- Ali Stewart

I remember the time Bopter asked me to go down to the Royals bar in Woodside as his sister had laid on a birthday party for him. We were in Murdo's bar at the time, so off we went, we walked in to a great reception from everyone and loads of birthday presents. Bopter stashed them all under a table, and after a while we went back up to Murdo's, great night and no trouble. Well, Bopter went back the next morning to collect his presents and to his surprise some fucker had stolen the lot.
- Ricky Sandison

"Market street got closed down until they got out of town. He was some guy just a machine." - Alan Low

"Some fuckin boy our big Bill. Mentioned in Jimmy Boyle book as the guy from Aberdeen he wouldn't mess with." - **Bruce Leslie**

One day I was standing in the Cavalier bar having a pint just minding my own business, I was only seventeen and just out of Glenochils young offenders. In walked this big blonde headed guy wearing a pin stripe suit and looking the part. He walked up to the pool chalk board, wiped all the names off and said, "I'm on next," it all kicked off with a load of this well-known boys. I watched in disbelief as Bopter knocked the six of them out. What amazed me was he kicked this guy straight in the face while he was standing up, I have never seen anything like it before. I was thinking, *there could only be one guy that this can be and that's this Bopter.* I had heard so much about him and was a legend to me. He was like lightning, and something out of a James Bond movie. What amazed me was after him knocking six of them out he picked up the cue, chalked it and said, "OK spots or stripes?"

The guy turned around with fear and said, "anything you want," the rest of them were all left lying on the ground.

Another day out with Bopter, we were in the Dancing Cairns and Bopter was playing a game of pool. In walked this up and coming Hard-nut and said to Bopter "Hey You! I'm on next." Well Bopter stuck the head on him and that was the guy finished.

Pub shut for the afternoon so we all went back to my house for more drink until the pub opened again. My brother Michael, Ronnie Boyle, Jim Buchan and myself were all sitting at a table while Bopter was playing pool again. The door opened and in walked the guy he had hit earlier on with about twelve of his mates. They walked past Bopter on their way through to the pool room and shouted, "Hey BIG man, you're going to get it soon!" Bopter finished his game of pool and then followed them into the pool room. I got up and said, "I better go and help Bopter" and as I walked through the fucking door, all hell broke loose and next thing someone had thrown a pool ball at my head and burst it wide open, blood pouring everywhere. I grabbed two pool cues and was screaming, "come on you bastards!" at that point Bopter was knocking most of them out, but me, I just wanted to kill them. It was some brawl, broken faces, arms, the lot! blood everywhere! I heard the police sirens and just headed for the door, and as I was walking out the police came running up towards me. I said to them "fuck me officers, I wouldn't go in there as I just went in for a drink and look what's happened to me," another lucky escape. We all ended up back at Jim Buchan's house to get cleaned up. Bopter said "Ok boys fancy going over to the Sunnybank Club for more drink?"

I said, "I can't as my shirts all covered in blood." Bopter threw me his suit jacket and said, "just wear this." (now remember Bopter's 6 feet 4 and I'm only 5 feet odds), I put it on anyway and headed over to the Sunnybank club.

The night went on and I was on the dance floor giving it a bit of this and that thinking I was so cool and looking over to our table as much to say Hey boys! look at me! and Bopter was grinning away to himself. I Got home and and looking in the mirror and to my embarrassment what a state I looked with this suit jacket on. I must have looked like a right knob dancing in the club. The moral of the story was I was more embarrassed at what I looked like than I was about that huge brawl we had earlier on in the day. - *Jim Robertson*

Jim Robertson and Bopter Macrae

CHAPTER 2

GONE BUT NOT FORGOTTEN

Small tribute to some of the men that could hold their own in their area of Aberdeen.

RODDY BAXTER

*"Remember when my Brother Roddy, Bopter and few
of their mates from Northfield was at the Beehive,
when up came this well-known Gang of the bikers to
sort them out. Within minutes Roddy and Bopter went
out and knocked the fuck out of them."*
- Poona Baxter

JOHNNY LESLIE

"Johnny Leslie, I was in jail a few times with him and he could well handle himself and also looked the part."
- Jim Robertson

"I remember the day when Johnny gave me a cockatoo bird as a present. Next day in the newspapers someone had gone into Hazelhead bird aviary and stole all the birds lol."
- May Turner

"Had many of chats with Johnny when we had our stalls down in the Castlegate, brilliant guy and never heard a bad word said about him, he would have given anyone his last."
- Mike Sheran

"Great guy had some laughs with him over the years"
- **Alan Low**

"Great lad always enjoyed his company."
- **Paul Dabell**

"What a great guy"
- **Karen Reid**

JOHNNY DYKER

"Johnny Dyker was a true tuff nut he didn't start trouble but if it came his way he could handle it well."
- **John Simpson**

"My dad told me that Dyker was scared of nothing and nobody and a cheeky chappy and a charmer."
- Marlene McLaughlin

"My da always said if you ever need someone at your back in a fight it would be Johnny Dyker he was fearless, that was his words."
- Steve Moore

"Johnny was on the deck of the trawler going out of the harbour and he asked a shipmate if he fancied a pint, the guy said where he said follow me and jumped over the side and swam up to the 19th hole pub dripping wet walked in and asked for a pint."
- Gordon McCallum

"Johnny Dyker was a legend"
- Ian Fraser

THE
CRUICKSHANKS

*"I was a good friend of the youngest brother Alex. I
didn't know the other brothers very well but had
heard plenty of stories about them being able to
handle themselves."*
- Mike Sheran

Alex wasn't the hardest in Aberdeen, but this guy was
the gamest guy I ever came across.

A true story I got told about him was when he was at Northfield
school and at that time the gang scene was very big. Northfield's
biggest rivals were the Mastrick Gringo! headed by Jim Robertson
and Co. One day they came up to Northfield school in two fish
trucks to have a go. The whole school kept their distance except
Alex who was challenging them to 'C'mon' but out of respect for
what he did the Mastrick lads just left him alone.

Another story I witnessed was one night up at Byron Square, these two Glaswegian guys appeared and pulled out two swords! Well, we all took to our heels, we couldn't see Alex, so we decided to go back for him. When we got back the two guys were out cold as Alex knocked them both out."

My pal Brian Cruickshank and I went into the Pavilion bar on Market street for the first time and that's where I got to know Bopter, Ginger, Larry Ford, Dod Moore and big Tommy Hardy. They were all playing three card brag, me and Brian had just done a turn so had a few pounds in our pocket. Well…. I got myself into their card game and after about ten minutes I noticed they were all cheating each other, being a bit mad myself I dealt the next hand and slipped myself three cards off the bottom. Well I won the hand and as I went to pick up the money big Tommy put his hands over mine and said, "not today son," I thought my life was coming to an end, but then he said for having the cheek to try and rip us off you won't get taken up the lane now so drink up and Fuck Off!... lucky boy. - *Ali Stewart*

"Alex always had your back"
- Mike Geddes

"Alan Cruickshank came back from London and I remember he used to walk about with a walking stick with a sword inside it. The four brothers have all passed away now great guy's but very dangerous."
- Karen Reid

"I loved that guy."
- Ronnie Boyle

111

CRUICKY

Walking home from the town one Saturday night and got to the top of Rosemount. I banged into Alex, Spesh and a few others. At that time, it was early eighties and we had no axe to grind with the Northfield lads because through football we were all pals now.

Anyway, we were all pissed and having the usual banter with each other and then Cruicky, produces a bottle of poppers, as if we are not all daft enough, so on we go up towards Midstocket. We hear music playing loudly from this bottom floor flat so it's certain we are going to gate crash. Andy Johnston decided to try the door, but it was locked. Cruicky wasn't having any of this and stuck his head in the window, he then starts to climb in.

There's a few words exchanged between Alex and the inside party, door now opens and out came this Bute wearing a waistcoat and a cravat, telling us to leave or he would get the police! Now all the party lot came out and then one stupid fucker grabs Alex. The wrong move as it all kicked off and they were all scrambling to get back in their house and we ended up getting lifted. Alex was a great guy, good footballer and someone who has left a great impression on all who met him RIP. - *Derek Hardy*

RAYMOND SEIVWRIGHT

Raymond Was a very well-respected man, and they say he had some punch on him. One day he was in town with his friend Norman Gardiner another guy, who could really look after himself, (but these two guys never looked for trouble.) But on this day a few guys started on them, wrong move! as they wiped the guys out. Next thing the coppers arrived heavy handed, there were about ten of them, but ten wasn't enough to sort Raymond and Norman out, so they had to adhere to spraying them with mace to control them.

One Saturday night in the early seventies Ray managed to get Amadeus nightclub shut down. Ray was minding his own business until one of the bouncers started with him, then one now became eight in total. One by One Ray knocked the eight of them out, lights went up and everyone was evacuated as there were no bouncers left to man the place.

Ray always said if you ever need anyone by your side, look no further than young Willie Stephen and his father Billy Stephen as they were both hardy fuckers.

"Ray was an absolute gem and could well handle himself but preferred to laugh and have fun and that was the real Raymond R.I.P"
- Brian Sutherland

"If you got a left hook from Raymond you would have known about it."
- Steve Moore

"Ray had the best left hook in Aberdeen also biggest heart ever. He gave me a few harsh words to sort myself out in my younger years and will never forget them. Legend is the only word to describe him."
- Iain Esslemont

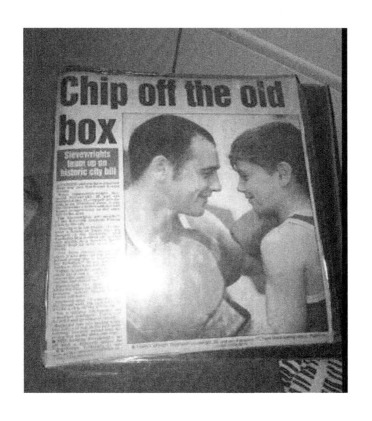

"Now that's history father and son fighting in the N.E on the same bill. Raymond Sievwright and Raymon Sievwright"
- Scott Sievwright

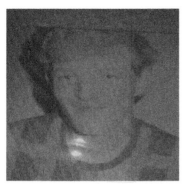 

MᶜPHEE BROTHERS

"John Mcphee, you couldn't have met a nicer bloke, he could have had a dash if he hit people, he broke bones."
- Sandy Flett

"No one messed with the McPhees."
- May Turner

"You had the McPhees and Alan Robertson all could handle themselves."
- Brenda Robertson

"I remember when Northfield Byron had a reputation and you could go anywhere without any hassle, my era we had Fatty and the pool room mob as the hard-nuts. My mob would have been a guy a lot of you will have known well that is Marco Mcphee one of the best."

"Marco went out with my best friend and never forget the first time she took him home to meet her parents. When Marco walked in the house him and my friend's father couldn't believe it as they had known each other, only because my friend's father was a Policeman and nicked Marco a few times lol."
- Arlene Chisholm

DENNIS & BOSCO ADAMS

"Will take a long way to beat Dennis and Bosco Adams from Torry for hardness and respect by others."
- Robert Mcdougall

"Now that was a real geezer."
- Max Thompson

"My old bouncer mate and friend."
- Dod Moore

"Another hard man of Aberdeen."
- Karen Thompson

117

"He looked after me in the Double Two in the seventies a true gent never to be forgotten."
- Brian Duncan

"Top-man"
- William Smith

"He was a legend."
- Debra Hay

"Great man"
- Brian Sutherland

LAWSON THAIN

"Another hard case I remember was Lawson Thain."
- Patrick Mcguire

GEORGE FRASER

PAT MENEHAM

"George Fats Fraser was a very good friend of mine and was fearless."
- **Gary Reid**

"Two of the best people I had the pleasure to call real friends Pat & Thora Meneham."
- *Bob Flinn*

PANDA

JIMBO GERAGHTY

RONNIE PIRIE

TERRY BRADY

JOHN CLARK

SHUGGIE MACNEILL

"John Clark, balls of steal and game as fuck"
- Wullie Stott

"Shuggie was a tilly legend."
- Scott Milson

120

MATTY MURRAY

**THOMAS
McDONALD**

JOHN BYRNS

**SCOTT
MONTGOMERY**

*"Knew John Byrne from the day I
moved to Fernie Brae, nice genuine
guy and never looked down on
anyone and would always be the first
to help."*
- Mike Sinclair

*"Scott Montgomery very good friend
and soldier to the end."*
- Joseph Merchant

121

CHAPTER 3

TRUE STORIES FROM SOME OF THE CHARACTERS IN THE BOOK

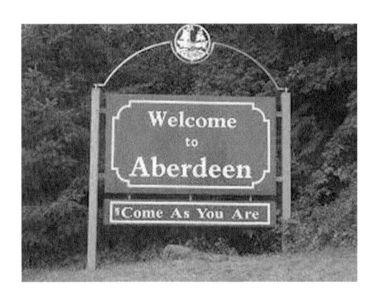

Hidden Identity

These stories have been revealed by people that have already been mentioned in the book, although names of the people included in their stories were given during interviews, out of respect and for legal reasons they will remain anonymous.

SHOTGUN AT MY 3-YEAR-OLD DAUGHTER'S HEAD

This drug dealer got a right doing over outside this well-known pub. He was then taken down to a bridge, held by his feet to dangle over it and threatened with a sword.

I was sitting in my house one day when the door got kicked in, and in walked these four Glasgow Gangsters. Each of them had been out on license as they were awaiting trial for murder.

They pulled out these guns and one of the pricks pointed it at my three-year-old daughter's head. He told me if I moved she was getting shot. They were told it was me who attacked their drug runner. One tied my hands behind my back, then the other one put his gun in my mouth. They then attacked me with knuckle dusters, and the butt of a shotgun. They gave me a proper doing in and I couldn't do a thing back as this guy was still pointing his gun at my daughter's head!

A few minutes go by and in walked this other guy He said, "boys! We have to go as we have got the wrong guy!" as they walked out, one of them said to the other guy "go on let me just take her eye out or rip her face." It was the scariest day of my life and I vowed to get them back one day. So, time went by and I was in jail again and this big Glasgow fucker said, "are you.....?"

I said "yeah, why?"

He said "the cunts that did that to you have all gone! Except for one of them! So, either you do him in or we'll do you in."

TILL THIS DAY DON'T KNOW
IF HE IS DEAD OR ALIVE

Me and a good friend walked into Wyness's pub on Exchange street. As I was heading towards the bar I looked over and noticed a group of people that I knew and hadn't seen for years. I went over to ask them what they would like to drink, I got their order and headed towards the bar, next thing this guy who was in their company shouted at me "hey I'll have a vodka!" I just ignored him, and as I got back to the table with their drinks, this guy in an 'aggressive manner' said "where's my fucking drink!"

My reply was "you're getting fuck all as I don't even know you!" the guy then picked up a glass and tried to smash it in my face. As I went for him, everyone held me back and said, "don't go near this guy, as he is one fucking evil cunt and he has just got out of prison after doing a very long stretch for either murder or attempted murder!" so then, the bar staff and the locals told me to leave as they were scared for my safety. All this happened around ten o'clock, I got outside and told my friend 'I'm not leaving until I get this fucker,' I told him to stay across the street and whatever happens not to get involved.

After about two hours standing in this doorway out the fucker came! I said "hello you remember me? You prick," then I just lost it.

My mate came across and pulled me off this guy and we headed towards Guild Street, 'His quick thinking,' he noticed a puddle and started to clean the blood off my hands and arms. I didn't know if I killed the guy or not. At that point there were blue sirens, flashing everywhere, cops and ambulance.

Again, his quick thinking was to give me his jacket. Two minutes after that, the cops pulled us up at the bottom off Exchange Street. As I looked up there was a crowd of people standing at the place where I left the guy lying in a pool of blood. The cops radioed up to the other cops and asked them to get the witnesses to look down and see if we fitted the description. Thank god they said, "No, because the guy that did it never had a jacket on." lucky escape!! And to this day I didn't know if I killed the guy or not.

I made such a mess of him and left him in a pool of blood. In all my fighting days it was the first time I had gone over the Top like that, but this guy was an animal.

FIFTY-FIVE STITCHES IN HIS HEAD

I was sitting in Flannies pub with a few friends of mine, and this guy had his head on the table next to me. My mate shouted on me to pass an ashtray, I didn't smoke myself but passed him the ashtray. This guy then lifted his head from the table and said in a threatening manner "put that fucking ashtray back!" so, I hit the fucker in the face with a pint mug, I picked his head off the table and slammed it back down. His two pals were there sitting at the table and never batted an eyelid. The guy ended up with fifty-five stitches.

THREW HIM OUT THE WINDOW

A friend of mine was in a bit of bother from this fucker who was staying down in a middle floor flat at Froghall. Off we went in a taxi to sort this guy out, I said to the guys that was with me "you lot stay down here, and I will fix him out on my own,"

I kicked the door in, slapped him about a few times and then I threw him out the window. He was lying there wriggling about with my friends looking up in disbelief.

I went across the room, picked up his TV and threw it out of the window after him. Luckily for me and the guy it missed him by inches if it hadn't it would have killed him.

HIT HIM THREE TIMES
WITH A BRICK

Back in the day when I was a youngster. I was a paperboy for Lintmill shops. There was this guy who was a couple of years older than me. Every Friday and Saturday he used to hound me, knowing that was the day I collected my paper money and my tips.

This went on for a few weeks, he would jump out from nowhere and empty my paper bag, kick the papers everywhere and choke the shit out of me until I handed over all my money.

One Saturday I saw him waiting for me. As I went to deliver a paper I emptied my bag in this garden and put this house brick in the bag. I started walking along the road and when he pounced on me, I let him have it. The first blow just registered, the second blow and he was on the deck! After the third blow he started screaming out of him.

Next thing this woman came out screaming at me saying she was going to phone the cops on me. 'Sod's law' this fucker had choked me and robbed me for weeks and this woman phones the cops on me.

GLASGOW GUYS CAME AT ME WITH
KNIVES

We had a private club of our own in the Broadsword bar. I was the bouncer there at the time and when the police came in we used to tell them to "Fuck Off!" as it was a member's club. These three Glasgow guys were in the pub this night and started mouthing off and singing Rangers songs. I went over and said, "keep it down boys and no singing your fucking football songs in this pub."

Guy turns around and says "aye nae bother big man"

I replied, "who you calling a fat bastard?" but they explained they say this to all men. Anyway, they behaved themselves all night, and came over to me, shook my hand and said, "thanks for a great night,"

My mate says "I'm just away to walk this lassie across the road, so I locked the door, minutes later a banging on the door. It was my mate screaming, "that Glasgow guys came at me with knives saying they're going to kill me!" I went out after them, wrapped my jacket around my arms and banged two of them that had the knives. The other one ran towards the Broadsword. I got hold of him, knocked fuck out of him and dragged his face along the brick wall, took most of his skin off his face.

EMPTIED THE ASHTRAY
INTO HIS MOUTH

Me and this well-known guy were always fighting with each other. Sometimes I would win! sometimes he would win! every time we saw each other we would end up fighting.

one night he phoned me from his flat and he was mouthing off because there were a couple of birds with him. I said to him "ok I will be down in a minute."

When I got there, I went running up the stairs and kicked his door in, out he came running towards me with a golf club in his hand. So, I stuck my head down and charged at him like a Rhino and he went flying. I noticed this ashtray, I picked it up and smacked him over the head with it and he was out cold. I then noticed another ashtray, which was full of fag ends and ash. I opened his mouth and tipped it inside and then walked calmly out of his flat and never had any more trouble or fights with him again.

THREW THE FUCKER
OFF THE TRAIN

On the train Coming back from a Scotland game, sitting having a game of cards with the boys and a few birds. This bird came in and started getting a bit frisky with me. So, me being a gentleman showed her where the toilet was. and that was me a member of the train version of the mile-high club lol, after a while these two guys came over and started with me because they found out what I was just up to with one of their birds. So, I knocked the first one out and made a right mess of the second guy. The train pulled up at Portlethen station, so I opened the door and kicked the fucker out before the train had stopped. My friend said, "what the fuck you doing? you're going to kill him."

My reply was "I think he is fucking dead anyway." The train now gets to Aberdeen and all we could see were cops everywhere.

My mate said, "change your top and put on this See You Jimmy! ginger wig and tartan hat," as the train stopped they carried me off the train to look as though I was pissed, and we walked straight by the cops I Found out later the guy wasn't dead, but he was in some mess.

PAID £500 JUST TO DO THIS GUY IN

I was sitting in the pub one day when this drunk fucker walked up to me and asked me to do in this guy for him from the Byron, for five hundred pounds because he was shagging his wife. I said "OK" so I met him at the Byron toilets. Next day he handed me an envelope with two hundred and fifty pounds inside, He said, "half now and half later when the jobs done,"

Well, that night the guy he wanted me to do in was playing pool with another well know hard nut from the bar. They got into an argument, next thing the guy from the bar made a right mess of this guy that I was paid to do in. Two days later I went into the Byron to meet the guy who paid me, and his words were "that's your other half of the money and what a great job you did on that bastard," he saw the guy walking down the street that morning with his face in a right mess thinking, it was me who did this.

BULLET JUST PAST MY HEAD

One of my friends was in a bit of trouble and asked for my help. He owed some Scousers money and these two Scousers were up looking for him.

At that point I had no fear and have never asked anyone for help I just sorted things on my own, anyway, I arranged to meet up with these Scousers under the bridge at Windmill Brae. When I got there, they were arguing with this guy who owed them money. I just stood back and watched, then I noticed one of the Scousers pull out a gun.

I started to walk towards him, the Scouser said "don't even think about it." I still carried on walking towards him when, he pointed the gun at me. He then fires it and with a bit of luck the bullet went past me. I ran towards him and rugby tackled him, then grabbed him by the nuts and squeezed as hard as I could so he couldn't use his hands because he still had the gun in his arms. I then managed to get my hand on his throat and pushed down on it as hard as I could until he passed out and then I just walked away, and nothing was ever said again.

TWELVE OF THEM ON TOP OF ME

I was at the bar watching the football with my brother and his mate, none of my mates were there that day. Off we went to the bar at opening time to watch Aberdeen v St Johnston in the cup. As the day went on we were knocking back the drink. Later on, a bus load of guys came back to the pub, after a while I looked over and seen this cunt looking over at me and giving me the dodgy eyes. I was thinking *what the fuck's that all about.* The guy then gets up and followed me down to my seat, I said to him "you all right mate? Is me and you alright? As you keep looking at me"

I was just making eye contact with him, just trying to make a joke of the situation, he said "who are you? And what's your name?"

I told him my name, he said "yeah, what's your surname?"

I knew at that point the guys looking for trouble as he was an arrogant cunt! I just carried on drinking, I went out for a smoke, well, out came this guy's mate, he kept asking for a puff of my fag, but I knew the guy didn't even smoke, so now, alarm bells were ringing. I'm thinking *he just came in the pub, with a bus load why didn't he ask them for a fag.* I ended up giving him a fag just to keep the peace. I went back in the bar to have a drink and all this lot were standing at the bar looking over at me.

After a while this Big Baldie fucker came over to me and said "Oi! Have you got a problem with my mate."?
I said, "who's your mate?" he pointed over to the guy in the red top that was asking me for a fag outside. At that point I flipped and said, "I canna be arsed we this and started raising my voice. Everyone was looking over, probably thinking what a dick head for raising my voice and kicking off. I said to the Baldie fuck! "You're trying to piss me off? Well, let's go! Me and you outside," he wouldn't come outside with me. Next thing the barmaid came over to me and said "sorry, but you're have to leave now."

I said, "I have been here all day minding my own business and this lot came in and started, and you're asking me to leave?"

I was fuming by this time, I walked up to the bar and said, "You! You! You! You! And You! Outside NOW!" Well, fuck me, the whole lot of them came outside, 'and' not just the five I challenged, I just grabbed the first one, let him have it and whoever next I got my hands on, just got it! After a while about twelve of them got me down and started kicking the shit out of me, but I was still grabbing legs and crawling over bodies that I laid out.

I managed to get up and floored a few more of them. I then got rugby tackled to the ground, then some fucker bit my neck, so I sank my teeth into someone's eyebrow. Not that I'm in the habit of biting people, but they started biting me.

I fight to survive and not just to win. This all happened at different stages and next thing three of them were on me, so I stuck my hand in this guy's mouth and tried to rip his mouth open. The guy is now screaming out of him and he ended up with half his ear missing!

The police arrived, they got me in the back of the van, covered in blood as my face was such a mess and I was screaming out "I'm coming back for the lot of you, and going to kill you all!"

So I was up in court and was told I'm looking at three years in jail. Got bail and went back to the pub to see if any of them were there, a couple of them met up with me later to apologise.

Up in court and I pleaded self-defence but was told it's only self-defence if you're in a corner and can't get out, but CCTV showed me going back for more. I couldn't believe it, they almost killed me and I was away to get jailed for it.

BIT OFF HIS EAR

One day my husband, a few family members and myself went into town for a few drinks. We decided to head to Charlie's night club and as we were passing the bouncers, my brother in law heard them making a snide comment about us. At that moment my brother in law didn't say a word in front of my husband, as he knew he would have attacked the bouncers.

When my husband decided to nip out for something, my brother in law then approached the bouncers. The next thing, all the bouncers were on top of him and threw us out!

I started shouting at this big 'coloured' bouncer. Me and my sister were giving him shit! At that point my husband walked around the corner and witnessed this big fucker slap me round the head.

Next thing, my husband attacked him and all I could hear was this bouncer screaming and crying out of him, because my husband had bit his ear off.

The police were all over the place and my husband took off down this road. The police then put me and my brother in a taxi. As I looked down I noticed the guy's ear, so I picked it up and put it in my handbag, in case they used it as evidence.

GET ME A KNIFE, SO I CAN CUT THIS FUCKERS THROAT

I was in Willie Millers on Hadden Street with a few of my mates, when a certain well-known guy from Tillydrone came in and bought all my mates a drink but left me out. I asked him why he did that, and he made some derogatory remark. Here we go again, both of us were at it again, no knockout until I fucked him over the head with an ashtray, then a knockout.

Another time I was in Willie millers, again when a few of my friends came in for a drink. After a while, we went up to the Villas nightclub as there was a punk night on. I went up to the bar to get the lads a drink while they, headed for the dance floor. Within seconds a riot had erupted, and we ended up outside. As I was speaking to my mate, I noticed my expensive jumper he was wearing was all fucking ripped! I asked him "who did that?" He pointed to this bodybuilder doorman. I approached him and shouted, "come outside you prick!" anyway, I gave him a bit of respect because he did. So, we went down to Windmill Brae and up this lane I smashed him a couple of times and turned him upside down, used his head as a battering ram against the cobbles. Then up-righted him, stretched his neck as far as it would go. I was screaming "Get me a Fucking Knife! So, I can cut this Fuckers Throat." My mates intervened and calmed me down.

HIS DOG WOULD HAVE TORN ME APART

I was friends with this guy who used to work for Mac Davidson the bookie. He was a toff, but he was a very nervous person. I would meet up with him on a Sunday and go up to the Cults hotel to meet up with other friends. There was this guy there, you could tell right away, he thought he was the 'Main Man' and nearly everyone feared him. My friend pointed him out and said, "every time I go into the pub this guy bullies me into buying drinks for him," sure enough this guy did look like an animal of a man, muscular build, and his shaved head.

I said to my friend "the next time he picks on you just let me know and I will come down and sort him out," Well, sure enough, a couple of weeks pass, and this guy was up to his old tricks again. My friend phoned me to tell me that he told the guy that I would sort him out!

I was in Troopers bar at the time. I waited about an hour for this guy to appear. Next thing the door gets swung open and in walked this guy with his mate with this BIG! Fucking! Bull Mastiff Dog! Which never had its leash on.

My heart sank to the ground, but the big mistake was that they never came over to me, they just went straight over to the bar. 'Thank fuck!' because that dog would have torn me apart.

I asked this other guy that was in the pub to shout the dog over, and whatever happens don't let the dog's collar go. As soon as he had the dog under control I marched over to the guy, stuck the head on him and knocked him straight out! And the funny thing was the dog I was more worried about didn't even bark once.

YANKED MY TEETH INTO
HIS LEG

I was out drinking with my two mates in the Clipper lounge pub. I noticed this two doormen, but never gave them a second thought, We left and went to the Moorings pub. We were waiting for our drinks and the two doormen from the Clipper lounge appeared next to me. One turned around to me and said that I was belittling him, I'm thinking. *Wait a minute, that's impossible because I only walked from Clipper to the Moorings and never encountered a soul,* anyway, I told the doorman he had got it all wrong. Well! Well! Here we go again.

He threw a punch which went flying past my ear, I thumped him and his sidekick and the next thing, I was on the floor, as the doormen from the Moorings joined in, thinking it was some free style competition with my body. I caught hold of a leg and yanked my teeth into it. I got myself up and out of the door.

I went up to the Mayfair pub where I bumped into an old friend of mine at the time. I was telling him the story about what just happened to me and as I was telling him the story, I was getting angrier and angrier. So, I decided to go back to the Clipper to make sure everything was OK. As I walked in I looked across the room, I saw one of the bouncers sitting on the stairs. The other fucker was standing next to the dance floor.

I lost it and I'm not sure what happened next, but one went for a sleep, and the other one followed, and all done with my tiny hands.

PROPER GANGSTER STUFF
BUT ALL TRUE

I was in jail with some serious Glaswegian gangsters who I became very good friends with, they liked me because I was a bit of a joker and just had a laugh with them. My time was just about up and only had a few days left before I got released.

They came up to my cell this day and asked if I would do a huge favor for them, they needed me to sort out this guy who was in a different part of the prison and they couldn't get near him, at that time my job was the gym pass-man and had access to most parts of the prison. I wasn't very keen on this until they told me what the guy was in jail for. So, I did what they asked but went a bit over the top.

Next morning, they came back to my cell and said "fuck me wee man you were only supposed to put him in hospital, but you just about killed him" I was questioned for two days about this incidence but they had no evidence against me. The Glasgow guys on the day I was being released gave me a contact number and told me if I was ever down that way to give them a call.

A year passed by and I was working on the oil rigs when I got a letter to say that I had been picked to play in a Piper Alpha charity match down in Glasgow against some of the Celtic Lisbon lions old team. It was to be held at a place called Helenvale park which used to be Celtic's training ground. I tried for a few days to get a hotel for the weekend but couldn't get one as it was the Glasgow marathon that weekend. I then remembered I still had that contact number of my friends in the jail. I Phoned the number and the guy that answered it was G. M who was one of my friends in jail, he just got released after a long stretch in

137

jail. "Oh fuck! he said how's it going wee man?" I told him about the football game and couldn't get a hotel.

He said "fuck me you're not playing in that game, are you? because it's our lot that is sponsoring the game.

I arrived off the train and waiting for me was a black flashy B.M.W and out jumped G.M and A.T, my two Glaswegian gangster friends from the jail. They took me to a hotel called the croft and had me booked in, told me they would be back at seven and for me to wear my suit. I got taken up to my room and 'oh my god!' what a place it had everything in it, en suite, balcony, etc.

Seven o' clock and I was outside waiting for them all dressed up in my new suit, black shirt and thinking I looked the dogs bollocks. They pulled up and burst out laughing and said, "fuck me who do you think you are fucking Al Capone?"

They took me to this Indian restaurant for a meal and a few drinks they told me that later on they were taking me to see this guy and I had to be on my best behavior, no laughing and joking and watch what I say in front of him.

They took me to this posh nightclub and when I walked in I noticed the guy Chris Quinton from Coronation street and Sam Fox sitting at a table, after a few drinks they took me upstairs to this office to meet this guy. I walked in and this guy walked over, shook my hand and just said "thank you" to me. He then said, "is your hotel ok? and is there anything else I could get you."

Me being a cheeky fucker said, "yeah, how about a couple of birds" lol. I found out later that the guy I had done in at the jail did something bad to this guy's granddaughter. That's the reason they looked after me in Glasgow. I went to the game on Sunday and we got beat 5-2 but I scored one of the goals past Ronnie Simpson the Lisbon lion.

CHAPTER
4

THE WOMEN

QUOTES FROM
'GROWING UP IN ABERDEEN-THE
HARD NUTS-PAST AND PRESENT'
FACEBOOK PAGE

THE FAMILIES

KINCORTH RIOT

THE WOMEN

Over the years Aberdeen has had its fair share of tough women, who could probably have sorted out half of the men, never mind the women. Some tough women I knew personally were Lynette Hutcheon, Poona Baxter, Debbie Watt, Karen Sangster and Big Dotty McLeod, you also had Brian Sutherland's sister Sally.

Hazel Robertson was also another, not a lot of woman would have taken her on, she did time better than Big Ben as she spent time in borstal, Cortonvale, and Craiginches prison, sadly she passed away at the early age of forty-two.

"I was brought up in East Tullos and back then no one messed with Jackie Duguid, not even the guys"
- **Mark George**

"Jackie was my personal welcome committee at Torry academy. I once asked her who put her in charge, she was shocked and told me later that my bravado saved me from getting my head kicked in"
- **Lyndee Robb**

LYNETTE

I remember when I was a kid about eight years old and it was knee deep in snow. I was out shovelling the snow and this guy started with me, I told him to 'fuck off' he said, "I'm getting my brother after you" so out came his brother, dived on me, and started choking me.

I picked up the shovel and smacked him over the head with it, the guy was never the same after that, he went to a special needs school and my mother used to say for years after that, it was my fault for hitting him over the head.

I moved down to Glasgow when I was about twelve and stayed there for a few years. I started to have many fights down there, one of my fights was against two eighteen-year-old women and I got the better of them both.

First day I went to Powis School it was half way through the first year, I was terrified and greeting to my da and he said, "you're going to fucking school,"

This girl said me "do you smoke?"

I said "yes" so we went to the toilets for a smoke. I had on this lovely new jumper, and the thing I hate is anyone saying, *oh geez a draw of your fag!* so this dame said to me, "geez a drag of your fag"

I said "no" so she flicked her lit tabby at me.

I said, "if you have marked my jumper your heads going down this toilet pot!" so that was me made my mark in school.

This well-known guy started with me in the corridor and later when he found out I was Sandy's sister, he could not have been nicer buying me sausage rolls and sweets. My brother Sandy was only there a week before he got expelled.

We were brought up as youngsters to never take shit from anyone and to stick up for ourselves even at sixty years old if someone punches me I will give them ten back. Most of my fights have been with men! on one occasion it was with my brother Sandy.

Sandy and myself went 'tattie' picking to earn some money in our pockets, we went into town one day, got as far as Bridge Street and the two of us were scrapping in the middle of the road, but Sandy always looked after me as I was the youngest in the family.

One day I was sitting at Broadsword bar when these two guys started on me, so I phoned Sandy and within minutes he was over to the pub and knocked the three of them out.

I was only about fifteen and it was the start of my drinking days. I went into town and borrowed my sister Val's new top, when she noticed what I had done she got hold of me in the middle of the town and ripped it off me and left me standing there with just my bra on.

TERESA MCPHERSON

Lynette told me that Teresa McPherson was the hardest woman she ever came across. Lynette's husband John was working as a glazier for the council when one day he had to fix some guys window. When he got there, he noticed someone was in the house. After time and time again knocking at his door still no answer, after about twenty minutes knocking this guy gently opened the door, he looked very worried. He told John to come in and explained why he took his time.

It was because he thought it was his girlfriend Teresa, he had a big argument with her the night before and she was going to throttle him! as John was fixing the window up pulled a taxi and this good-looking woman with blonde hair wearing a red suit stepped out.

John shouted out to the guy, "Hey your girlfriend hasn't got blonde hair and wears a red suit, does she?" the guy started to shit himself and was shouting at John to call the police. The police arrive, and it took six policemen to lift Teresa out of the building;

Teresa McPherson and her father Bobby who was also a hard nut and spent most of his early years fighting in the boxing booths.

"Not much people took on my sister Teresa" - Angela Jamieson

POONA BAXTER

"No recognition of the females lol ,,,, so I thought I would add this woman , back in the days and probably still stands her own..... my mother used to tell me how off the scale she was. But massive heart without saying."
- **Trish Ellis**

"I have known Poona for most of my life , such a nice person and great sense of humour , she would have needed to be after spending years with that 'numpty' of hers lol. Northfield lass, brought up with all her brothers and was also brought up to stand up for herself."
- **Mike Sheran**

FACEBOOK GROUP

Growing up in Aberdeen The Hardnuts Past & Present, is a Facebook group that was created to unite people people from Aberdeen and allow each individual to share their stories and opinions on who they might have regarded as an 'Aberdeen Hardnut'. Here are some of the comments that were posted on the group.

Elizabeth McEwan - My brother Willie Sim, a hard man back in his day, I remember when I was young and there was this man they called the 'rubber ball' and he challenged my brother to a fight, so Willie walks up to him and says to him 'oh so they call you the rubber ball, well I'm going to make you bounce all over the place' it took Willie one slap to finish him off and that man bounced no more.

Ali Stewart - Take it from me that guy 'Willie SIM' was not one to mess with, but never a bully or a liberty taker he was a toe to toe man and glad to say one of my very good friends from Froghall.

Jim Buchan - Great pal of mine back in the day and Willie could sure handle himself. Willie could fight for fun, a quiet guy and not a trouble maker never fought in two's or hunted in packs like some, he stood alone like his father before him.

Bri Sutherland - We also had big Charlie Small who was no man's fool I remember when we use to walk up Manor avenue and none of us would open our mouths when he passed, just the way he looked at us was enough. Met him in the Regent bar a few times and just a gentleman.

Alan Ford - Dodd McQueen was very handy he was small with curly hair and quietly spoken but his punch was like a sledgehammer.

Stan Clark - Brian Wood, Ackie Benzie, Bertram Boys, Spider and Ronnie Ritchie.

Heather Thompson - Arthur Davidson from Sandilands.

Willie Burnett - Ronnie and Dod Ritchie who run the White Horse pub in Woodside, they never took a backward step, against anyone.

Steven Kelly - Keithy Hall, he had a heart like a lion and would fight anyone.

Patrick McGuire - Bobby Reith was another hard case.

Dod Moore - Dod and Ronnie Ritchie from Seaton.

Jim Forbes - Ronnie Taylor was a trawler-man and lost a couple of fingers caught in a hatch, true gentleman and you would have never thought he was as hard as nails.

Phill Marshall - Daryl Senior followed in his father's footsteps.

Dod Moore - Dick McGregor who worked as a bouncer in the Cheval casino he was a right hard-man.

Arlene Chisholm - Young Eric Cameron and his dad was a hardy bugger.

Donna Leslie - My old man Davie Watt was a hard nut in his time drank a lot with Bopter and Jim Robertson.

Patrick McGuire - Jimmy Gordon from Froghall another hard case.

Barry McDonald - Wallace booth and Ally Nelson 50s and 60s real hard-men for sure.

Simon Butler - Another one was Matthew Boyle back in his days.

Willie Stott - Raeburn from Torry was pretty handy.

Brian Reid - John Thornton was a handful back in the days.

Dod Moore - Miller's bar you had Jim and Tam brown.

Jim Thompson - Graham Moir from Woodside was top man and some machine.

Karen Cargill - Old Joe McGunnigle, some man and his sons Gary and Joe. A good family a decent reputation and could carry themselves with respect.

Brian Sutherland - I met some nice people over the years, also met some right tuff nuts that most of you would not know and some you will. Tom Riley, Sandy Hutcheon, Sean and Keith McIntyre, Malcolm Aldridge, Stan Noble, Neil Lovie, Gordon, and Billy Duguid, just to name but a few Tom McKay big dandy.

Ricky Sandison - Larry Anderson was a tough nut 100%.

William Smith - One of the hardest guy to come out of Torry was the Gadgie.

Dennis Fairhurst - What about Fruggle from Northfield who had a metal plate in his forehead, I watched him fighting one day outside the Byron chip shop when this guy hit him over the head with an old-fashioned thick cider bottle, (big mistake), Fruggles head split wide open but no blood because of the metal plate, Fruggle ended up kicking ten ton of shit out of him.

Dingle Kids – Not trying to be bias, but one person we think should have a mention in this book is our Da, Michael (Fatman) Sheran. Many a fights over the years, bare-knuckle style. He hates bullies and has always said that trouble always came to him, he never went looking for it. (although us three might be on his hit list now as we've sneaked this comment in before being sent to the publisher) One thing for sure, if any of his friends or family were in any bother he would be the first one to the rescue, He would do anything for anyone. Our Da is and always will be our 'Aberdeen Hurd-nut'. One thing we know for sure, he is a well respected 'Northfield Loon' and we're sure most people that know him would agree. Even though he's a Grumpy Git most of the time, We're very proud to call him our Dad!

Patrick McGuire - Another hard case from Torry was Eky Pee.

Venessa Cox - Yan Esson now that man had some hit on him I have seen many guys he knocked out, also Ronnie and Dod Ritchie another two hard men.

Steven McPhail - You had Thumper, Neil McClellan. Frankie Lonie, Dave Nicol, Govie, Tojo, Mike Davidson and Brian Milne just a few of the Kincorth guys.

John Masson - In my days Ernie Flood was the hard man in Logie Avenue area.

Lulu Smith - Another two hard-nuts was Billy Horne and his wife Marion who battered guys, she was a stunner and you would think butter wouldn't melt in her mouth.

Mike Bain - Joe Gills grandson Jim Moore is another hardy cheil from Torry – The Balnagask Bomber.

George Woods - Nobody messed with Ronnie Taylor. Jock Cruickshank and Colin Lawrence were another two hard nuts, you also had Max Davidson who became Aberdeen's top bookie. George Johnstone who was known as the Sea Basket, he was one of the real hard-cases of Aberdeen. Once he carried a motorbike on his shoulders all the way up to the top floor in his building.

Away back in the day I knew a lot of the hard guys. In my days in the forties and fifties I was the best of friends with a lot of guys mentioned, most of them were trawler-men who I sailed with except Max Davidson who was a bloke that took shit from no one, the rest of them Ronnie Taylor, Billy Duguid and Colin Lawrence, they were always together, they would go to sea drunk come home get their pay cheque go and get drunk again and then head up to the dancehall Locarno's in George Street, and guarantee they would get into a fight lol.

Ronnie wasn't scared of anyone and all the time I saw him fighting he always came out the winner. Now, Andy Lawson, he was the same a proper hard-case, he was the bouncer in the Locarno and when he was on the door everyone behaved themselves.

GEORGE WOODS

Mike Sheran - One night in town Billy Stephens and a few of his mates Alec and Sandy Gibson, Jerry Summers and Yan Esson was walking up Market street when a group of six guys started on them, they ended up knocking the six of them out and the cops were phoned but they were scared to go into the pub to lift them, so Billy and Yan went outside and ended up knocking the six coppers out as well. Another time Billy was drinking in the 19th hole pub and a big fight started, someone threw a glass at Billy but it just missed him so Billy went off on one and the tables in the pub was screwed down but Billy still managed to rip it up and throw it at them and he cleaned the whole bar out, Alan and Larry Ford always said that Billy was the man to have on your side as he was no man's fool.

BILLY STEPHENS

Mike Sheran - I had known Sandy from my days working in the fish, sandy would come down a few times to visit his sisters Lynette and Val. He would always chat away to me and never came across as a 'Hard-nut', but the amount of people that have told me that Sandy was one of the hardest men in town . He never looked for trouble but by fuck if it came his way he sorted it out.

Fred Munroe - Haven't saw Sandy in years, hard as nails but never a bully. I worked with Lynette when she was fifteen … lovely people.

SANDY HUTCHEON

Some of the well-known and respected families in Aberdeen, that you didn't want to get on the wrong side of.

Lumsdens - McGregors - Stewarts
McPhersons - McAllisters - McDonalds
Sims - Andersons - Algie's... etc .

BENNY AND JIMMER LUMSDEN

A list of some people that have not been mentioned, but were able to handle themselves.

Northfield... Bob Murrison, Jimmy Townsley, Willie McGuire, Danny Harrison, Gappy McGregor, Rob Reith..Etc

Byron Pub... Kipper Heslop, Wilkie, Bob Flinn, John Ross, Walter Senior, Young Alan Robertson...Etc.

Other areas... Kenny Dunbar, Biffo, Bover Beatie, Vince Cairns, Goves, Brady's, Mike Moir, Fulhar, Mike Davidson, Larry Ford, Tom Riley, Ginger McColl, Ronnie Taylor, Ali Nelson, Jac & Ronnie Main, Ronnie Ritchie, Sean & Keith McIntyre, Stan Noble, Max Davidson, Arthur Davidson, Charlie Walker, Malcolm Aldridge, Wallace Booth, Neil Lovie, Beefy, Jimmy Gordon, Dod Mathieson., Jock Cruickshank, Dod Thain, Jim Gray, Akie Benzie, Brian Wood, Colin Lawrence, Gordon Shand, Eddie Greig, Ronnie Walker, Gordon Westland, Dennis McDonald...Etc

WALTER SENIOR

LARRY FORD

SOME TEAM OF HARD
FUCKERS BACK IN THE DAY

KINCORTH RIOT 1978

June the 3rd Scotland v Peru, I worked offshore and was making good money at the time, we were in my bedroom watching my little coloured TV, which was very rare to have at that time. We were all drinking snake bites and I made a statement that if Peru scored again, the TV was going threw the window. Well, Peru scored so I picked up the TV and threw it right through the glass window.

My mates were saying, "What the fuck are you doing? that's a new coloured TV!" My brother and Gary Mitchell left the house first with our carry out followed by Ally Strachan and myself. As we were walking up to the Covies pub I heard a BANG, CRASH! and thought *fuck me, has my brother dropped the carry out?* We turned the corner and Oh my God! this guy was attacking my brother with a hammer! It was about 9.15pm and I ran towards the guy, dived on him, pinned him to the ground and put his arm up his back, I then slammed his head off the ground and burst his nose wide open. My brother picked up the guys hammer and started hitting him on the back with it, I was telling my brother to get to fuck and grabbed the hammer off him, next thing this woman was shouting out her window, "Oi! you're the cunt that just pissed in my lobby, my husband's coming down to get you!

I replied, "Fucking tell him to come down now!", but she just told me to, "Fuck off!" and closed her window.

We're now at the Covies and I was in the bar with my mates because there was a disco on in the lounge. There was a commotion outside with Mike Davidson and a group of people. Someone came in and said, "Neil, the cops are outside looking for you," two coppers came in one was called Bill McKenzie, he approached me and said, "Neil have you got a minute?" they asked me what happened so I told them about the guy and the hammer and they asked me to go down to the station with them. My reply was, "like fuck I will because I know you lot, take me down there and lock me up till Monday!"

They said, "Ok, but could you come out and speak to us in the van?" I went into the van and one of the coppers started taking a statement, I told him exactly what happened, when he went out the van he left one door open, I could see outside and the next thing I could hear my brother screaming, "You black bastards!" another two coppers had pulled him from outside the pub and he started with them. I could see part of it through the gap in the door, my brother was getting the better of the two coppers, when a third copper appeared and pulled a baton out and started laying into my brother with it. I leaned back and booted the back of the door, unknown to me sergeant Mackenzie was behind the door and he just fell to the ground and was out cold, so fuck it, me and my brother ended up kicking the shit out of the three coppers.

A few police vans pulled up with about twenty coppers wearing riot hats and shields, they started to fight with us. One of my mates ran into the pub and shouted, "C'mon boys, Neil and his brothers are fighting with the coppers!" everyone came running out and then a battle began. What made it worse was all the teenagers had just come out of the chip shop topped up with cider etc. and they got wired in as well, they were running about with coppers hats and walkie talkies. The police dogs were let loose on us and Mickey Davidson hit a dog over the head with a pole and ended up killing it.

More and more coppers arrived, so everyone started to run off and I managed to slip past them, but finally they caught me and were screaming, "That's the bastard! Get him!". Apparently, some of the coppers that turned up were stinking of drink.

I was caught on Leggart Avenue and thrown in the van. They cuffed my left hand to my right leg and cuffed me to the back of the van, they then threw me out the van, I landed on my back and they dragged me along the street, bouncing off the road while I was still attached to the van. When they got me back inside the van I was such a mess and one of the coppers said, "You OK son?"

I said, "yeah but I'm all sore," he went Bang! full force on my face and said you are now you cunt!" They drove me down to the police station and when they opened the doors, A sergeant looked into the van and said, "What the fuck has happened here?" one of the coppers response was, "Oh this is the cunt that started the riot" the sergeant screamed at him, "I don't give a fuck who started it! Get him to the hospital now!" I remember my mate Tommy Campbell say to me, "Neil, Neil! Stay awake and don't let this cunt get the better of you!"

My face, head and eye were burst open, my ear was cut, I lost my top lip, 3 back teeth and three pints of blood, I was in a critical condition in intensive care and was just about dead! My solicitor tried to get into the hospital to take pictures of me, but they wouldn't let him in.

This old woman was in court for my defense as she witnessed them dragging me behind their van.

Pf "What did you See?"
Witness "I was watching TV and heard this noise outside, so when I looked out this man was being dragged along by this police van. Then they picked him up and threw him in the van and drove away."
Pf "Oh, Mrs., can you remember what you were watching on TV at the time and did you have on your glasses?"
Witness "Oh yes," she replied
Pf "Mrs. do you have more than one pair of glasses?"
Witness "Oh yes, I have glasses for driving"

Her evidence was thrown out because she had her TV glasses on when she looked outside, and she could have been mistaken for thinking I wasn't thrown out the van but fell out. They asked the hospital if it was possible if I had fallen out the van and my jeans were caught up on the door and that's why I was dragged along the road and used that as evidence.

The way the jury looked at me, I knew I was going down for a long spell. I was charged with three police assaults, one serious assault, breach of the peace, mobbing and rioting. I got Two years for assault, two years for mobbing and rioting, one year for police assault and six months for breach. Five and a half years in total, the judge said if it was up to me, I would have given you ten years as you are nothing but an evil despicable character.

When my mate Gary Ingles was up in court the judge said to him, "Mr. Ingles, why did you kick the police officer who was laying out cold in the middle of the street?"

Gary said, "Well, I thought he was sleeping and kicked him to wake him up" LOL, the court burst out laughing, the judge said, "So you did kick him?" and gave him twenty-one months in jail.

We got sent to Craigie and the rest was sent to young offenders. When we were marched down the hall to our cells all the cons were singing, we were like heroes to them because we did the coppers in.

Twelve of us in the dock for the Kincorth Riot and this is very weird, the six guys that were in the back row are all dead now and the six older ones in the front are all still alive. It was the longest trial in Scotland for years.

THE FINAL WORDS

I would Like to take this opportunity to thank a few folk...

My kids, Lee, Michelle and Kerry for their hard work with the publishing, etc,
Everyone on our Facebook group, you have all been brilliant and I couldn't have done this book without you.
Everyone who has taken the time to let me interview them, honestly, you have all been great and I have loved every minute of it!
Jill Robertson for all her help setting up some of the interviews.
Gift That Bottle Facebook page for making everyone in the book a little keepsake.

As for the book, some will like it, some might not, but all I can say is I tried my best.

These comments say it all...

"This has been one awesome memory trip, these Facebook group pages have been fantastic at meeting blasts from the past and I have found myself laughing smiling at some of the comments. My heart filled with happiness. Knowing sure that we are all the same. A group of nutty individuals with the biggest hearts, loyalty and respect. When we were growing up I never looked at any of these people with fear, they all had one thing in common and that was the word respect. We grew up safe, nothing was ever going to come over us to this day I raise my glass with respect." - **Karen Cargill**

"History in the making its great for the Aberdeen area, that they may have held their own, but had the utmost respect for their own elderly people and those that had nothing were helped out one way or another."
- May Turner

**THIS BOOK IS DEDICATED
TO GOOD FRIEND'S
WHO SADLY PASSED AWAY DURING THE EDITING
PROCESS**

R.I.P

Val Hutcheon

Darren Wright

Printed in Great Britain
by Amazon

34448776R00098